A
LADY
AT THE
TABLE

OTHER GENTLEMANNERS™ BOOKS

How to Be a Gentleman
John Bridges

A Gentleman Entertains
John Bridges and Bryan Curtis

As a Gentleman Would Say
John Bridges and Bryan Curtis

A Gentleman Gets Dressed Up
John Bridges and Bryan Curtis

A Gentleman at the Table
John Bridges and Bryan Curtis

A Gentleman Raises His Glass
John Bridges and Bryan Curtis

A Gentleman Pens a Note
John Bridges and Bryan Curtis

How to Be a Lady
Candace Simpson-Giles

As a Lady Would Say
Sheryl Shade

How to Raise a Lady
Kay West

How to Raise a Gentleman
Kay West

A LADY AT THE TABLE

A Concise,
Contemporary Guide
to Table Manners

SHERYL SHADE

WITH JOHN BRIDGES AND BRYAN CURTIS

RUTLEDGE HILL PRESS
Nashville, Tennessee
A Division of Thomas Nelson Publishers
Since 1798

www.thomasnelson.com

For Alma Mazer, Christy Thomas,
and the women of Alpha Delta Pi

Published by Rutledge Hill Press, a Division of Thomas
Nelson, Inc., P.O. Box 141000, Nashville, Tennessee 37214.

Library of Congress Cataloging-in-Publication Data

Shade, Sheryl, 1958–
    A lady at the table : a concise, contemporary guide to table
manners / Sheryl Shade with John Bridges and Bryan Curtis.
        p. cm.
    ISBN 1-4016-0177-4
    1. Table etiquette. 2. Etiquette for women. I. Bridges,
John, 1950– II. Curtis, Bryan, 1960– III. Title.
    BJ2041.S53 2004
    395.5'4—dc22

                                                2004016967

Printed in the United States of America

04 05 06 07 08—9 8 7 6 5 4 3 2 1

CONTENTS

Introduction   vii

37 Things Every Lady Should Know
Before She Comes to the Table   1

1. FROM COURSE TO COURSE   7
    Knives and Forks, and How to Use Them

2. A LADY FACES HER FOOD   51
    Skillful Maneuvers at the Table

3. SERVING AND BEING SERVED   79
    A Lady at a Private Dinner

4. IN THE PRESENCE OF OTHERS   101
    Dining at a Restaurant

5. THE JOB OF EATING   157
    Business Meals, All Day Long

6. STAND UP AND BE FED   167
    Cocktail Parties and Buffet Suppers

7. THE GHASTLY TABLE   181
    Dealing with Dining Disasters

INTRODUCTION

When a lady comes to the table—whether it is a formal dinner, a business luncheon, or a casual get-together—she may feel intimidated. The utensils and the plates will be arrayed before her, and she may even be offered unfamiliar foods. Years ago, it was simply assumed that any lady was well-trained in the intricacies of table manners, either because her mother had passed down that knowledge to her, or because she had received special training in etiquette classes. Such assumptions no longer persist, but even the best-intentioned lady may find herself wishing that she had paid better attention when her mother said, "Remember, when eating your soup, you always keep the bowl of the spoon turned *away* from you."

This book will help remind a lady of her mother's sound advice—or it may teach her things that her mother never thought to tell her. Because social entertaining has become so casual, a lady may wish to brush up on her manners after accepting an invitation to a formal dinner. What's more, because increasing numbers of women are in leadership positions in the business world, she may wish to do a bit of homework before hosting a meal in a restaurant for an important client.

Perhaps her mother was never faced with the challenge of ordering a bottle of wine, figuring the tip on a large restaurant bill, or dealing with a less-than-competent server. But a lady may now expect to encounter such situations on a fairly regular basis. She knows how to treat a server with respect, but she also knows how to stand her ground and say, "Please give the check to *me*."

Despite all the changes in the world, however, a lady knows that there still can be no more memorable experience than a well-prepared meal, shared with longtime friends or pleasant new acquaintances. Her role may be that of the gracious hostess or that of the grateful guest, but in either case she knows her job is to help the occasion proceed as smoothly as possible.

This book is filled with the details of the dinner table, but it also offers the knowledge that will help a lady feel self-confident at any breakfast, luncheon, or social event. A lady recognizes the value of knowing which spoon or fork to use, but she also knows that, whatever the occasion, when she comes to the table her goal is to enjoy the company of others so that, in the end, she will also discover that she has enjoyed herself. With the guidance provided by this book she will find herself equipped to pass along the right advice to her own daughter—or maybe even to her son.

37 Things
Every Lady Should Know
Before She Comes
to the Table

A lady does not "grade" the table
manners of her fellow diners.

——

A lady does not assume that her fellow
diners are "grading" her own behavior.

——

A lady does not
talk with her mouth full.

——

A lady does not chew with her
mouth open, nor does she smack
her lips, no matter how delicious
her food may be.

——

A lady makes as little noise
as possible while eating.

——

A lady does not chomp on ice.

——

A lady does not pick her
teeth at the table.

——

A lady keeps her napkin in her lap
while she is eating.

——

A lady sits up straight,
especially at the table.

——

A lady keeps her elbows off the table
when a meal is under way.

——

If a lady finds that she has
bread crumbs on her blouse,
she brushes them off.

——

A lady finds no need to
apologize for bread crumbs.

——

A lady does not play with
her food, kneading her bread with
her fingers or stirring the last
uneaten morsels of her dinner
about on her plate.

——

A lady does not
lean back in her chair.

———

If a lady is asked to pass the salt
or pepper, she passes them both.

———

A lady does not leave the table
without asking to be excused.

———

When a lady leaves the table,
she need not explain her reason
for asking to be excused.

———

A lady tries her best not to
belch or burp at the table.

———

If a lady must belch or
burp at the table, she covers
her mouth with her napkin.

———

A lady knows that belches, burps,
and coughs can occur at any time.
She keeps her napkin ready to
muffle unfortunate sounds.

———

37 THINGS EVERY LADY SHOULD KNOW
BEFORE SHE COMES TO THE TABLE

A lady need not use her
handkerchief to stifle a slight
sneeze, cough, or burp at the table.
Instead, she uses her napkin.

———

If a lady finds herself in a
situation, such as a fit of sneezing,
that necessitates the use of her
handkerchief, she leaves the table.

———

A lady *never* blows her
nose at the table.

———

A lady says please and
thank you, especially to servers,
in a restaurant or in a private home.

———

A lady does not wolf down her food.

———

A lady does not slurp her soup.

———

A lady does not
eat more food than she can
comfortably digest.

———

A LADY AT THE TABLE

4

A lady does not attempt to
cool her food by blowing on it.
If she fears singeing her taste buds,
she lets her food cool gradually and
undisturbed in its own bowl or
on its own plate.

———

Whether she is an invited guest
or the host of a restaurant party,
a lady shows up on time.

———

A lady does not apply
makeup at the table.

———

If a lady is offered a second
helping, she may accept it
if she wishes.

———

When a lady chews,
she chews quietly.

———

A lady shows up at the time of
her reservation at a restaurant.

———

If she is given the
opportunity to serve herself,
either at a family-style dinner party
or at a buffet, a lady does not
overload her plate.

———

A lady never argues with a
server, whether at a restaurant
or at a private party.

———

A lady does not overstay
her welcome. However, she may
linger at the table after dinner, along
with the other guests and her host or
hostess, knowing that such moments
are often the most pleasing and
satisfying of the evening.

———

In any aspect of her life,
but especially at the dinner table,
a lady does not bite off more
than she can chew.

———

1

From Course to Course

Knives and Forks, and How to Use Them

When she sits down at the table, a lady surveys the equipment set before her, just as a doctor makes sure she is equipped with all the instruments to be used in surgery. Of course, using the wrong fork for the salad or reaching for the incorrect water glass is not as disastrous as selecting the wrong scalpel. But a lady realizes that not knowing her way around a dinner table can throw off the dynamics of a meal, leaving her on pins and needles and in constant fear of embarrassing herself. The good news is that with a little practice, a lady can maneuver her way around any table—be it at a Sunday luncheon at her grandmother's or a formal dinner at the White House.

If a lady discovers that her
napkin has slipped from her lap to
the floor, she retrieves it, if she
can do so gracefully.

————

If the retrieval of her napkin
threatens to disrupt the dinner
table, a lady simply turns to her
host or hostess and says, "I'm
afraid I've dropped my napkin.
May I have another?"

————

If a lady is served meat
in a private home and is not
offered a steak knife, she does not ask
for one, lest she embarrass her host
or hostess (who may not own steak
knives or who may assume she has
found the entrée too tough to
cut with a dinner knife).

————

Once a lady has finished
stirring her cup of coffee, her cup of
tea, or her glass of iced tea, she places
her spoon on her saucer. A lady
never places a damp or soiled
utensil directly on the table
or the tablecloth.

—

If a server offers freshly
ground pepper for a lady's soup,
salad, or entrée, the lady may accept
the offer or decline it, no matter
what her dinner companions
choose to do.

—

A lady does not chop up her
salad with her knife and fork before
proceeding to eat it. If the salad is
not served in easily eaten pieces, she
cuts it into one bite-sized piece at a
time, as she eats it.

—

At some elegant dinner
parties, a scoop of sorbet (usually
citrus flavored) will be served
immediately after the first course or
after the entrée. A lady does not
assume that her dessert has already
arrived. She recognizes this touch
of cold tartness as a "palate cleanser,"
intended to give her taste buds
a rest eitherbefore or after
a heavy entrée.

—

Unless she is confident in her
knowledge of china, porcelain, and
other ceramics, a lady refers to the
plates set in front of her as "dishes."
She knows it is always wiser to err
on the side of simplicity than
on pretentiousness.

—

Two Forks in the Road

When a lady sits down to a meal—breakfast, luncheon, or dinner—she usually finds that the necessary flatware has been provided. (A truly thoughtful host or hostess never puts out more than two forks or knives at the beginning of a dinner, as a greater number of utensils might be intimidating and confusing, and unnecessarily clutter the table.)

A lady will find the knives and spoons arranged on the right side of her plate and the forks on the left side. On all occasions, a lady assumes that she begins by using the utensils farthest from her plate. This means that when she is presented with the first course, she uses the fork and knife farthest from her plate. Once that course has been completed, she leaves that course's utensils (fork, spoon, or knife and fork) on her plate. As each new course arrives, she simply uses the utensils that are closer and closer to her plate.

Only one general exception to this rule exists. When a lady sits down at the table, she may find a small fork placed on the right side of her plate, outside the knives and spoons. This tiny fork is called a shrimp fork or a cocktail fork, and is intended for use with a first course or an appetizer consisting of shrimp or other shellfish. Shrimp forks are seldom encountered these days. They remain, however, the only forks ever placed on the right side of the plate.

For the most part, when a lady sits down at a formal dinner, she may look at the table and clearly anticipate what lies ahead. If she sees two forks on the left side of her plate, she assumes that she will be offered at least two courses during her dinner. Any time her plate is changed or a new course is presented, a lady assumes that she is to move along to another fork, knife, or spoon.

Should a lady discover that she has run out of knives or forks before the last course has been served, she feels perfectly comfortable in quietly telling the server, "I could use another knife [or another fork]." She does not apologize.

If the utensils have been provided out of order and a lady uses them in the order in which they have been provided, the server is at fault, not the lady. A lady never corrects her host or hostess, nor does she correct a server employed by another person. Instead, especially at a private home, she follows the lead of her host or hostess. Her role in the dinner, after all, is to be a gracious participant. She refrains from any behavior or comment that might make her dinner companions uncomfortable.

When Salad Is Served
as a First Course

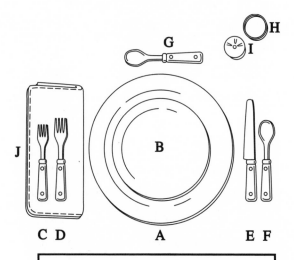

A. Dinner Plate	**F. Teaspoon**
B. Salad Plate	**G. Dessertspoon***
C. Salad Fork	**H. Water Glass**
D. Dinner Fork	**I. Wine Goblet**
E. Dinner Knife	**J. Napkin**

The dessert utensil can be a fork if appropriate.

When Salad Is Served
Along with the Entrée

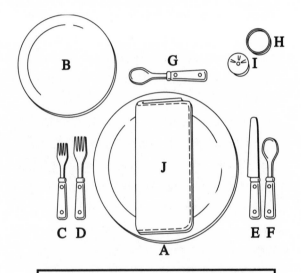

A. Dinner Plate	F. Teaspoon
B. Salad Plate	G. Dessertspoon*
C. Salad Fork	H. Water Glass
D. Dinner Fork	I. Wine Goblet
E. Dinner Knife	J. Napkin

The dessert utensil can be a fork if appropriate.

THE CHAIR LADY

Even in today's more egalitarian society, and even in the business world, a lady may well discover that the gentleman seated next to her, or the server in a restaurant, intends to help her with her chair. In no case does a lady assume that the gentleman is condescending to her or that he figures she is incapable of seating herself. Instead, as the gentleman pulls out her chair for her, she slips in and says, "Thank you so much." The gentleman will keep his hand on the back of her chair as she slides it closer to the table, but she takes it upon herself to set the chair in the position that is most comfortable for her.

When she leaves the table for any reason, the gentleman may again offer to assist her with her chair. She may either accept his help, saying, "Thank you," or she may simply say, "Thank you, but please don't get up."

At any large social event or in a restaurant, a lady may choose to briefly leave her place at the table to greet friends at other tables. She knows that when she approaches another table, even for a brief hello, the gentlemen at the table may stand up to greet her. Thus, she does not linger. Again, she is thoughtful enough to say, "Thank you, but please don't get up."

A lady should not be surprised, however, if no gentleman rises to assist her when she arrives at the table. In fact, if she is seated next to an elderly person—or even a gentleman who may be having trouble with his own chair—it is *her* responsibility to offer to help with the chair.

THE NAPKIN

When a lady takes her seat at a formal dinner, or at a table in a restaurant, however informal, she immediately unfolds her napkin (even if it is made of paper), and places it in her lap. In this one case, she does not wait for her host or hostess to lead the way. If a lady must use her napkin during the dinner to blot her lips or wipe her cheek, she does so, always returning the napkin to her lap.

If a lady must leave the table for any reason during a dinner, she simply leaves her unfolded napkin on the seat of her chair. (A lady never leaves a used napkin on the dinner table until the final course has been served and she has finished her meal.) In some upscale restaurants, after she has correctly left her napkin on her chair, she will return to the table only to find that a server has refolded her soiled napkin and returned it to the table.

In such cases, no matter how fine the restaurant, the server—or the policy of the restaurant—is wrong. A lady never puts her used napkin on the table until she has finished her meal. She waits, in fact, until the dinner party is obviously coming to a close, and then places her unfolded napkin on the table as a declaration that she understands that the dessert has been served, no more coffee will be offered, and no more wine will be poured.

If a lady is the hostess of a dinner party, she places her used napkin on the table to signal the official end of the party. Guests may linger at the table as long as they like, but they may not expect any further food or drink to be served. The hostess, however, may suggest, "Why don't we move along to the living room [or to the den] for coffee [or an after-dinner drink]?" In such cases, the guests simply leave their napkins on the table and proceed to the other room.

A lady does not fret if she soils her napkin over the course of a dinner party. She understands that napkins were created to be used—not to be kept clean.

Finger Bowls

After she has finished her entrée, and especially after an entrée such as ribs or lamb chops that may have soiled the lady's fingers, a clear glass bowl of warm water may be set directly before her, on a saucer. Alternatively, the bowl may be set at the left side of her service plate. She will probably discover a sliver of lemon or a few rose petals floating in the water. The lady recognizes this bowl as her finger bowl, and she dips her fingers quickly into the water, brushing them with the lemon slice or the rose petals, if she chooses, then quickly dries her fingers with her table napkin.

After a particularly challenging side of ribs or a rack of lamb, a lady may be presented with a clean, steaming towel, with which she discreetly wipes her fingers, and even her mouth, before the next course arrives. After she has used this towel, a lady returns it to the plate on which it was presented.

When dining in a restaurant, such as a steak house, that specializes in entrées that may be eaten with the fingers, such as ribs or rack of lamb, a lady feels perfectly comfortable in asking the server for "a warm towel."

The Fork and Knife

At any breakfast, luncheon, or dinner a lady will be presented with two primary utensils: a fork and a knife. Depending upon the formality of the occasion and the number of courses being served, she may be offered more than one fork and more than one knife. She may also be presented with one or more spoons. But the business of dealing with the basic utensils does not vary—from course to course, from meal to meal, or from table to table.

A lady will always find her knife at the right side of her plate. If the knife is placed correctly, its blade will be facing toward the plate—a tradition based upon the assumption, for good or ill, that most ladies are right-handed. If a right-handed lady picks up her knife, with the blade turned toward the plate, she may plunge right into her dinner. A left-handed lady will no doubt have developed her own means of coping with the challenges of almost any occasion, culinary and otherwise. In no case does a lady make a scene by examining the cleanliness of her utensils. If she discovers that one of her utensils is less than spotless, she simply asks for a replacement. She never attempts to polish it with her dinner napkin.

Dinner Knife

The dinner knife is the
standard knife with which a
lady will be greeted when
she sits down at any table.
Occasionally, she may also
be faced with a fish knife
(see facing page), which
suggests that she will be
served fish as a first course. If
two dinner knives are set
before her, and if a first
course is served, a lady uses
the first knife, farthest to her
right, for her first course. If a
lady has been served a course
and she has run out of
knives, she simply says to
the server, "May I have
another knife, please?"

Fish Knife

A lady recognizes a fish knife because of its wide, scallop-shaped blade, which is useful for cutting tender, flaky fish. If a lady sees a fish knife set beside her plate, she assumes she will be served fish as an appetizer or a main course.

Steak Knife

Steak knives are generally available in restaurants, and there a lady may ask for one. In a private home, however, a lady never asks for a steak knife. She fears that her host or hostess may not have steak knives readily at hand, and she also does not wish to offend her host or hostess by implying that the chop set before her is too tough to cut with a dinner knife.

Butter Knife

A lady finds her butter knife, also known as a "butter spreader," set on her butter plate, just above her forks, at the upper left-hand side of her plate. She uses this knife to spread butter or jam or jelly on her bread. It has no other function.

Dinner Fork

The dinner fork is the standard fork with which a lady will be presented when she sits down to dinner at any restaurant or any private dinner. If she is offered more than one dinner fork, she uses each of them as each new course is presented. However, if she sees a salad fork or a shrimp fork (see pages 27 and 28), she uses them in the manner described.

Salad Fork

Somewhat shorter than a dinner fork, the salad fork has wider tines, which make it easier for the fork to pick up slightly greasy, perfectly dressed greens. Although salads are sometimes served as a first course, a lady may also find them served after the entrée. A lady leaves the salad fork alone until the salad is served.

Shrimp Fork

Also known as a "seafood fork" or a "cocktail fork," a shrimp fork is only provided when a lady is served an appetizer of cold fish, shellfish, or mollusks. Unlike any other fork, the shrimp fork is set down at the right of the lady's plate.

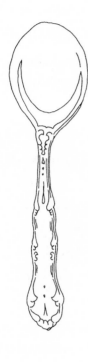

Soupspoon

A lady will find the all-purpose soupspoon at the right side of her plate. It informs her that she will be having soup as one of her courses.

This spoon may also be called a "dessertspoon." If it is intended to be used for dessert, the spoon sits above the lady's plate. She will recognize it because it will sit horizontally above her plate.

Teaspoon

If a lady sits down and finds a teaspoon set before her, close to her dinner plate, she does nothing with it, unless she is offered tea or coffee later in the evening. If she is offered tea or coffee, she uses the teaspoon to stir it gently. (She does not use her spoon to dip from the sugar bowl; she uses, instead, the spoon provided with the sugar.) In most cases, however, her coffee will be accompanied by its own small spoon, as will her tea.

Iced Tea Spoon

A lady uses the long-handled iced tea spoon to stir sugar and other sweeteners, lemon, and lime into iced tea, iced coffee, and other iced drinks. This spoon comes in handy because such drinks are usually served in tall glasses.

THE "BANK DINING ROOM SALAD FORK"

At luncheons in the dining rooms of some large gray-suit corporations, a curious dining-room tradition persists: The salad fork (the fork with shorter, broader-spaced tines) is placed inside, closer to the plate than the fork for the main course, even though salad may be served as a first course. Because a lady assumes that for her first course she will use the first fork available to her, this tradition has led to unnecessary discomfort for generations of uncomfortable job applicants. In such situations, a lady simply follows the lead of her host or hostess.

THE MULTITASKING LADY

A lady may use her fork and knife in either the American or the Continental style. In the strictly American style (see page 34), she uses her knife and fork to slice a bite of meat or vegetables, then places her knife on her plate and switches her fork to her right hand. In this style, a lady uses only her right hand to feed herself, making sure to keep the tines of her fork turned upward. (The process, although illogical because of the utensil switching involved, is not as elaborate as it sounds, and is the process most Americans have been taught as children to use.)

The Continental style (see page 35) is much more convenient—and is the style many ladies find themselves using, no matter how they have been trained by their mothers. In the Continental style, a lady uses her fork with her left hand at all times, just as she found it on the left side of her plate. After using her knife and fork to slice a bit of meat or vegetables, she places her knife on her plate. She transfers her food from plate to mouth using her left hand, with the tines of her fork turned downward.

A lady may use either the American or Continental style, anytime she wishes. She need not conform to the behavior of anyone else at the table—not even her host or hostess—in regard to this matter.

The American Style

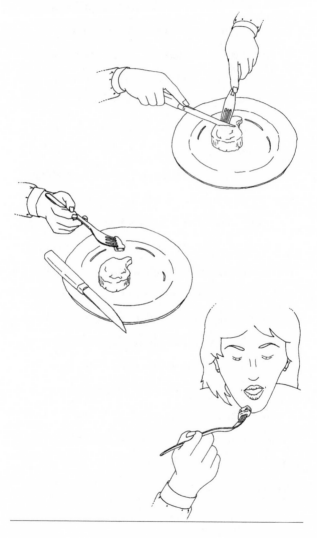

The Continental Style

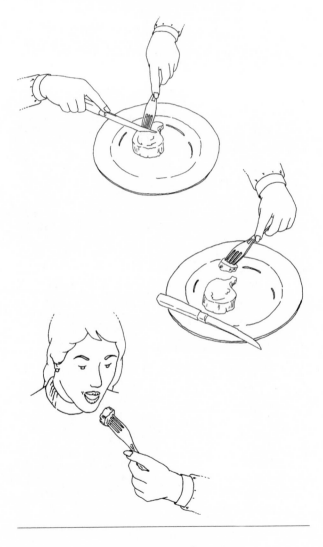

How to Use Chopsticks

At many restaurants offering Asian cuisine—particularly those featuring sushi, sashimi, and stir-fry—a lady may find herself presented with a pair of chopsticks as her only utensils.

The use of chopsticks is not a complicated maneuver. Here is a simple guide.

1. The lady places one chopstick in the crease of her thumb.
2. She braces the other chopstick against her ring finger.
3. She uses the two chopsticks, as if they were tweezers or pliers, to pick up bite-sized portions of food, dip them in soy sauce or other condiments, and then pop them into her mouth. (Sushi and sashimi are usually served in bite-sized or two-bite-sized portions.)

If a lady is not comfortable using chopsticks, she asks the server, "May I have a knife and fork?"

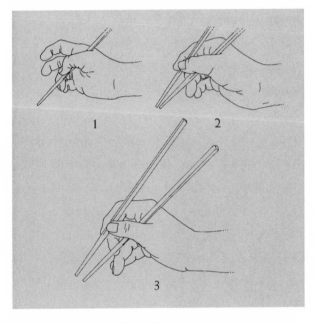

The Plates

When a lady sits down at a well-planned dinner, she will find that, along with the knives, forks, and spoons, a dinner-sized plate has been set at her place. This is her service plate. It is preset on the table so that the lady and the other dinner guests never sit down to a bare table, and it remains on the table until the entrée has been finished. It may, in fact, turn out to be the plate on which her entrée is served. In some cases, a lady will find that her dinner plate has been preset on an even larger plate, made of china, pottery, or polished metal. This large, almost shield-sized plate, is known as a "charger." Its function is largely decorative, but it also helps prevent dribbles of food from splashing onto the tablecloth.

The lady may discover that her napkin has already been placed directly on her service plate—in which case she removes it immediately and places it directly in her lap. Or she may find that the salad course or appetizer has already been set out, on its own plate, atop the service plate.

At an intimate dinner party (a table of eight or fewer people), once all the guests are seated she waits until her hostess begins to eat, before beginning her own meal. If she is the only lady at the table, however, it is her responsibility to lift the first fork or spoon, so that the gentlemen at her table can feel free to follow suit.

At a large party or banquet, where more than eight people are involved, she may feel free to begin eating as soon as the guests on either side of her have been served. She knows that if she waits until a dozen people—much less two hundred people—have been served, her soup will grow cold or her salad will grow limp.

On some occasions, such as luncheons or casual dinners, a lady may discover that her salad plate has been placed just above her forks, at the upper left side of her service plate. In such cases, she assumes that she will be expected to eat her salad as an accompaniment to her main course.

GLASSWARE

Across the course of time, cups and glasses have been specifically designed or developed for virtually every possible beverage. A lady learns to recognize them so that when she sits down at the table, she already knows what she will be offered to drink during the evening.

Water Glass
The water glass is large enough so that it will not need to be refilled with great frequency. It may also be used for iced tea or soda.

White Wine

A white wine glass has a long stem and a slender globe. The shape has evolved to keep the drinker's fingers away from the glass so that the wine stays as cool as possible. The tall glass does its best to prevent the tart liveliness of the white wine from evaporating.

Red Wine

The red wine glass serves precisely the opposite function from that of its white wine brother. The globe of the red wine glass has a wide shape so that it may be coddled in the hand, allowing the wine to be subtly warmed by the touch of a palm.

Champagne Flute

The elegant champagne flute helps preserve the bubbles of the exquisite, celebratory wine for which it is intended. Its delicate shape helps contain the champagne's effervescence.

Highball

The tall, cylindrical highball glass is useful at any bar or party. It can be used for iced tea, soda, or any combination of liquor and a "mixer" (which means tonic water, soda water, cranberry juice, orange juice, or any other non-alcoholic beverage). The mix of a liquor and a "mixer" is what makes a drink a "highball." If the drink consists entirely of liquors, as with a martini, then and only then is it called a "cocktail."

Old-fashioned

The squat, thick-glassed old-fashioned is the preferred glass for drinks of undiluted liquors, such as Scotch on the rocks or a martini on the rocks. ("On the rocks" means simply that the liquor, or mix of liquors, is served over ice, as opposed to being served "up," without ice.) The old-fashioned takes its name from one of the great cocktails of the 1920s and '30s, a mixture of bourbon, bitters, orange, and sugar, combined with a splash of soda and served in a short glass.

Double Old-fashioned

The taller, double old-fashioned has become the classic cocktail glass. It may be used for iced tea, for a soda, for vodka mixed with tonic, or for any other simple cocktail. It provides more room for liquid, or liquor and mixer, than a simple old-fashioned allows.

Brandy Snifter

The snifter was created to be cradled in the palm, because brandy—which warms the soul and body—glows even more warmly when held in the gentle grasp of a caressing hand. Its balloon-like shape allows the aromatics of a brandy or liqueur to aerate, but it also concentrates the delicious perfumes through its narrowed "mouth." A snifter of fine brandy is the perfect, comforting close to a lovely dinner, but a lady takes care when treating herself to more than one.

Liqueur Glass

Set on a slender stem, the small liqueur glass (also known as a "cordial glass") is used for after-dinner drinks such as crème de menthe, Bénédictine, or amaretto. Especially if the glass is more bowl shaped, it may also be used for an after-dinner wine, such as port.

Demitasse

A lady may be presented with a demitasse—a straight-sided, miniature coffee cup containing extremely strong (perhaps flavored) coffee—at the end of her dinner, most likely when dessert is served, or when chocolates are passed in the lingering time after the actual dinner is done. She may either accept or decline a demitasse. She may request decaf if she chooses, but a decaf demitasse obviates the shock of caffeine, which is the reason this tiny coffee cup was invented.

Finishing Up

When a lady has finished any course of her meal, she leaves her used knife, fork, or spoon on the plate, or in the bowl from which she has just eaten. She never places a used utensil directly on the dinner table. When a lady has finished her entrée, it is traditional to place her knife and fork, side by side, on her plate, to indicate that she has finished eating. She places her used utensils on the lower right-hand side of her plate, pointing toward the center of the plate as shown in the illustration.

A lady may then expect a server, or her host or hostess, to take away the dinner plate, removing it from the right side of the lady's place at the table.

If salad has not been served earlier during the meal, a lady may expect that it will be served now.

At some particularly gracious dinner parties, a platter of cheeses, perhaps accompanied by fruit and bread or crackers, may be offered after the salad course but before dessert. Port may be served to accompany the cheese course. After a heavy meal involving a cheese plate, a lady does not expect a flamboyant dessert. Instead, she expects to be served a selection of chocolates or small cakes and tarts, accompanied by coffee, brandy, or liqueurs. At this point in the evening, if a lady feels she has already been plentifully served, she may simply say, "Thanks, but I believe I'll just have another glass of water."

If there is no cheese course, dessert follows directly after the entrée. In such cases, it may be accompanied by a dessert wine, champagne, or coffee. When a lady first sits down at the table, she may find that a spoon, a fork, or a spoon and fork have been set directly above her plate. If no dessertspoon or fork has been preset, she is confident that it will be provided whenever the dessert is served.

It is traditional for servers to remove each diner's plate as soon as it is empty, or as soon as that diner indicates that he or she has finished with that particular course. This practice means that the diners are not left with their dirty plates staring up at them. (A lady indicates that she has finished by placing her knife and fork side by side on her plate, as explained previously. Alternatively, the server may ask her "Are you finished, ma'am?" to which she responds, "Yes, thank you," or "I think I'll finish the last couple of bites.")

Nowadays, however, a lady may ask that her plate not be cleared away until all her fellow diners are finished. Her intention, of course, is that no lonely diner will be left to finish a meal while the rest of the diners stare down at the empty tablecloth. When dining with four or fewer people, a lady may do as she pleases at this moment in the dinner. When she is a guest at a larger party, she is well advised to follow the example set by her host or hostess.

Place Cards and Menu Cards

When a lady arrives at a dinner party, she may discover that place cards have been set out on the table. She understands that her host or hostess will have given some thought to the arrangement of the guests. She also understands that her host or hostess will have consciously decided not to seat her next to her spouse or her date for the evening, as it is assumed that there will be other times when the lady can enjoy that person's company.

A lady feels free to check out the seating arrangement, even before the entire party is called to the table. If she discovers that she has been seated next to a person whose company she does not enjoy (perhaps even a guest with whom she has had a recent argument), she may ask her host or hostess if her place card may be moved. (She does not take it upon herself to rearrange the carefully planned table.) The host or hostess may agree to make the switch, or the change of place may require a reseating of the entire table—a complexity the host or hostess has no time to deal with at the last minute. If that turns out to be the case, a lady simply bucks up and makes the best of the evening, knowing that the dinner will be over within an hour or two.

Once she is seated at her table, a lady may find a menu card, outlining the courses for the dinner or luncheon, in front of her plate or between her and her closest dining companion. A lady feels free to pick up the menu card and examine it, but she always puts it back on the table where she found it, so that it serves its purpose for others at the table.

2

A Lady Faces Her Food

Skillful Maneuvers at the Table

A lady understands that eating is a craft, a craft that sometimes requires finely honed skills, special tools, and unflagging attention to the job at hand. A lady should never feel threatened by any dish that is put before her, but she will be wise to acquaint herself with the tabletop challenges discussed in this chapter. She may encounter some of them, such as a plate of escargot, only on the rarest of occasions, but she may be treated to a bowl of fettuccine at any moment, and on any day or evening she may be faced with a wedge of lemon. Squeezing a lemon wedge, she thinks, is a simple enough task, but she surely can remember times when she has sent a spray of lemon juice sailing into a nearby diner's eye. To avoid even this sort of annoyance requires forethought and a bit of acquired skill.

A lady never calls attention
to another person's poor table
manners, unless that person is
her own child.

—

Unless she foresees a disaster,
such as an overturned soda or a
spilled bowl of soup, a lady does not
correct the manners of even her own
child while in the presence of
non–family members.

—

If a lady is dining in a restaurant
and has not been provided with
the proper utensil for the food set
before her, she asks her server
for it immediately.

—

If a lady is hosting an event
in her home, she provides the
proper utensils for the dishes she is
serving. If a lady does not have the
proper utensils, she adjusts her
menu accordingly.

———

A LADY AT THE TABLE

The Breaking of Bread

A lady may expect to find bread—a hard roll, a soft roll, a slice of sourdough, or bread of any type—offered to her at any luncheon or dinner gathering. At a restaurant or at a private club where she is a guest (at a large wedding reception or rehearsal dinner, for example), she simply tells the server, "We'd like some bread here, if you please." When the breadbasket arrives, she says, "Thank you." If she sees that bread is not being served at other tables in the room, she does not ask for it.

At many restaurants, banquet halls, or private dinners, a lady will be furnished a bread plate. She will find this bread plate—a small plate, perhaps with a small knife set across it—set above the forks, at the upper left hand of her luncheon or dinner plate. The knife set across her bread plate is her butter knife. She uses it to spread butter on her bread. A butter knife serves no other purpose during the course of any meal.

If a breadbasket is passed from person to person, at any dinner or luncheon, public or private, a lady takes a roll or a slice of bread from the basket. If the bread slices are slender or the rolls are small, and if the lady is particularly hungry, she may take more than one slice of bread or more than one roll. She does not, however, help herself to more than one piece if by so doing she would empty the breadbasket. Neither does she "stockpile" rolls or slices of bread, as if she will never eat again.

At a dinner table, when a lady discovers that the breadbasket has been placed directly in front of her or within her easy reach, she does not hesitate. If she chooses to do so, she takes a roll or a slice of bread from the basket, places it on her bread plate, and then passes the basket along. If a plate of butter pats, or butter in any form, is provided, she takes what she pleases and passes it along as well. A lady passes bread and butter, or any other dish, around the table clockwise, which means that she passes it to her left.

At many fine restaurants, society dinners, and swell private parties, bread may be served, but a lady may discover that no bread plate has been provided. She may come to the table only to find that a large roll has been placed directly on the table, at the left side of her plate, just above the forks. In most situations, this will be the only bread she will be offered throughout the first course and the entrée. Once a lady has begun eating this roll, she places it on her plate. A lady never places even a bit of gravied or buttered bread on the tablecloth. She does her best not to soil the table linen.

When a lady is served bread, she actually "breaks" it before consuming it. Whether she has taken a roll or a slice of bread, a lady always breaks her bread into a bite-sized portion, one piece at a time, as she eats it. Doing otherwise, of course, might allow bits of bread to go dry upon her plate. She butters each morsel of bread, or dips it into the olive oil, seconds before she intends to pop it in her mouth. Even with a freshly baked roll, a lady resists the temptation to slather the entire thing with butter, as she might inadvertently find her fingers covered with grease after every bite of bread. In the privacy of her own home, a lady may indulge in such pleasures, but she does not allow herself these private indulgences in front of others.

In the Soup

In many households and at many formal dinners, soup is offered as the first course. The soup bowl or cup will be placed directly in front of the lady, on her service plate. Crackers or toasted bread may be offered along with the soup, and she takes them if she wishes to do so.

When eating soup, a lady always uses the spoon to scoop away from herself, thereby reducing the likelihood of dribbles. If she wants to enjoy the final spoonfuls of soup, a lady tips the soup bowl up and away from her, to make it easier to scoop the soup into her spoon. Once she has finished her soup or consumed as much of it as she desires, she returns her spoon to her bowl.

Should a lady be served a soup, such as shrimp bisque, that she cannot eat because of an allergy, dietary restrictions, or any other reason, she has two options. She may simply place her spoon in her soup dish and enjoy a few crackers or a bit of toast. Or she may decline to take any soup at all. If she is asked, "Is there something wrong with your soup?" she simply replies, "It looks beautiful. I just don't eat shrimp."

THE TERROR OF THE TEA BAG

When a lady orders a cup of tea in a restaurant, she will most likely be provided with an empty cup (usually with its own saucer), a tea bag, and a small pot of hot water. In short, she will be provided with the equipment necessary for her to brew her own tea.

She proceeds to place the tea bag in her cup and pours the hot water over it. After she has allowed the tea to steep for three to five minutes (the longer it steeps, of course, the stronger it will be), she removes the tea bag from her cup and places it on her saucer. If no saucer is provided, she places the used tea bag on the rim of her bread plate. If no bread plate is provided, she has no option except to place the tea bag on the rim of her dinner or dessert plate. In no case does she squeeze the bag against the rim of her teacup, as if she were attempting to extrude the last dribble of flavor. If a lady wishes to add lemon and sugar to her tea, she adds them after she has removed her tea bag from the cup.

28 Challenging Foods and How to Eat Them

Be it a wedge of cantaloupe served in its rind at a restaurant, or corn on the cob and fried chicken served at a picnic, a lady never knows when she will come up against a dining challenge. While the temptation when eating alone is to do whatever is easiest, a lady knows that when dining in the presence of others there are rules to be followed. A lady never finds it tedious to follow such rules because she knows that they exist to make her life easier and maybe even a good deal less messy. This list offers guidelines for some tried and true techniques of the table.

Artichokes: If a lady is served an artichoke, it will usually be served to her whole, its leaves pointing upward. A lady pulls each leaf off, dips it in the sauce (if a sauce has been provided), and scrapes it between her teeth to remove the tender flesh. Once all the leaves are gone, a hairy little island will remain in the middle of the artichoke. This is the "choke." A lady uses her knife and fork to slice it away, uncovering the delicious artichoke "heart" underneath. She cuts the heart into bite-sized pieces and dips them in the sauce before eating them. A finger bowl may be placed on the table so that she may clean her fingers.

Asparagus: If asparagus is served cold, without any sauce, a lady may eat it with her fingers. If she prefers, she may use her knife and fork, of course.

Avocado: A lady may sometimes encounter an avocado, unpeeled but cut in half, and topped with some filling, such as chicken or seafood salad. In such cases, if the avocado is sufficiently ripe, she uses her spoon to scoop out the tender, creamy green flesh. If the avocado is underripe, however, she does not attempt to eat it at all, since both its texture and its taste are sure to be unappetizing. If a lady encounters cubes of peeled avocado, as part of a salad, she eats them with her fork.

Bacon: If bacon is crisply cooked, a lady may eat it with her fingers. If the bacon is still a bit limp and greasy, she uses her knife and fork.

Caviar: Caviar is most often served as an hors d'oeuvre, heaped on crackers or toast, or spooned into scooped-out new potatoes. It may, however, also be served as a first course, presented in a small dish set in a small bowl of ice, with crusts of bread and a variety of traditional accompaniments, such as grated onion, sieved egg, and capers. A lady remembers that caviar is salty and that a little goes a long way. She uses her napkin carefully because black fish eggs can make an ugly stain.

Cherry tomatoes: A cherry tomato may prove to be sweet and juicy, any time of the year, but its juiciness can lead to problems. Whether she encounters one in her salad or on her dinner plate, a lady spears the cherry tomato with her fork. If it is bite-sized she pops the whole thing into her mouth. If it is too large to consume in one bite, a lady uses her knife and fork to cut it in half. She never simply bites into a cherry tomato, for fear of squirting her fellow diners with juice and seeds.

Corn on the cob: Corn on the cob is almost never served at a formal dinner or in an upscale restaurant. But even at a picnic, a lady butters her ear of corn carefully. She spreads the butter along a couple of rows of kernels and then picks up the ear, using both hands. She bites off the kernels, working from one end of the ear to the other. She then butters another couple of rows and proceeds in the same fashion.

Crab: To get the maximum amount of meat—and the maximum pleasure—from a crab, a lady first uses her fingers to tear off the legs. Then, making as little noise as possible, she sucks out the meat. Next, she breaks open the back (a small hammer may be provided; otherwise, she uses her knife and fork) and removes the meat with her fork. (If she is lucky, a small fork will have been provided for this purpose; otherwise, she uses her dinner fork and the tip of her knife.) A soft-shell crab is entirely edible, and may be eaten with a knife and fork.

Escargot: If a lady encounters escargot (the French term for edible snails) at a dinner party, she will be provided with the equipment necessary for eating them. A special pair of tongs to grip the snail and a small fork for pulling the meat out of the shell will be provided. The tiny shellfish fork is placed on the right side of the plate, outside the knife and spoon. If no tongs are provided, the lady must use her fingers to hold the shell. She makes sure to get a good grip. Otherwise, the rounded shells may go sailing around the room.

French fries: In a casual setting, a lady simply picks her french fries up with her fingers, or she may choose to use a fork. She attempts not to slather her fries with ketchup or other sauces, lest she dribble the sauce on the table or on herself. If the fry is too large to be consumed in a single bite, the lady does not put the half-eaten piece back on her plate. Instead, she keeps it in her fingers or on her fork until she is ready to eat it. If a lady and other diners are sharing a dipping sauce, she pours a small pool of the sauce on her plate, replenishing it as the need arises. She does not dip her fries into the communal sauce bowl after every bite. A lady does not double dip.

Fried chicken: Although fried chicken is a delicious American classic, a lady will rarely encounter it anywhere except in the most informal of settings, such as picnics, at-home dinners, or very casual restaurants. In these settings, it is perfectly correct to eat the chicken with her fingers. Using the fingers is, in fact, much more convenient than attempting to cut the meat from the bones with a knife and fork. Whenever she eats anything with her fingers, of course, a lady makes frequent use of her napkin. A boneless breast of chicken, whether fried, baked, or grilled, is another matter entirely. A lady always eats it with her knife and fork.

Grapefruit: If the grapefruit sections have not already been loosened from the rind, a lady removes the fruit using a grapefruit spoon, which has a serrated edge, if one is provided. Otherwise, she uses her knife and fork to loosen the sections. She conducts this procedure very carefully, however, to prevent squirting the juice on her fellow diners or on her own blouse. If necessary, a lady uses her utensil-free hand to steady the grapefruit. Once the flesh of the grapefruit has been separated from the rind, she eats it with her grapefruit spoon or with her fork, whichever has been provided.

Grapes: If the grapes are served in clusters, a lady picks up the cluster and eats the grapes with her fingers. If the grapes are removed from the cluster and served as a garnish, she may eat them with her fingers or spear them with her fork. If the grapes are part of a fruit salad, she always uses a fork.

Gravy: If a gravy or sauce is served along with any course, a lady serves herself, using the ladle or spoon accompanying the bowl or gravy boat. She pours the gravy or sauce directly on the food for which it was intended.

She does not use it to drown everything served on her plate.

Lemon or lime: A lady will often be offered lemon, either cut in half or served as wedges, to accompany beverages, seafood, or vegetables. At some dinners, and at many restaurants, a lemon half will arrive tied up in a piece of fine-mesh fabric. This "bootee" is intended to prevent lemon seeds from splattering over the lady's food or onto the plates of her fellow diners. In any case, whether she is squeezing lemon into her iced tea or over her salmon steak, a lady squeezes it with one hand, using the other hand to shield herself and others from the spray of citrus juice.

Lobster: A delicacy for some, lobster can also be a disaster if a lady does not know how to handle it. Because eating lobster can be an extremely messy ritual, it is one time when a lady may protect herself with a napkin tucked into her blouse front. In some restaurants, she may even be offered a bib. Here is the technique for attacking a succulent lobster:

1. Twist off the claws. Separate the sections of the front claws at each of the joints.

2. Crack the claws with nutcrackers (which will be provided in restaurants or homes where lobster is served). Use a pick, as needed, to remove the flesh from the claws.

3. Twist the tail from the body.

4. Remove the tail flippers from the tail.

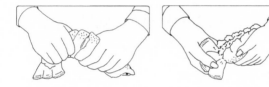

5. Using a fork, push out the tail meat.

6. Remove the shell from the body of the lobster.

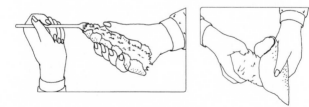

7. Remove the smaller claws.

8. Using a pick, a fork, or even your teeth, remove the meat from the smaller claws.

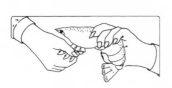

Melon, served in the rind: A lady uses her knife and fork to eat any melon that is served in its rind—whether watermelon, cantaloupe, honeydew, or any other variety. She makes vertical cuts in the flesh of the melon, slicing almost down to the rind. She then slices across the upper edge of the fruit, thus cutting it into bite-sized cubes that may be tidily eaten, using her fork. If the melon has already been cubed, the lady simply eats it with her fork.

Oysters, clams, and other mollusks, served on the half shell: A lady firmly grips the shell in one hand and, using her cocktail or oyster fork, spears the delicious morsel. If she wishes, she dips it into any sauce that is provided. A lady eats any oyster, clam, mussel, or other mollusk in one bite. In an informal setting—such as an oyster bar or a party among close friends—she may pick up the shell and sip the juice, known as the "liquor."

Pasta: When faced with a plate of pasta, a lady resists every temptation to chop it up with her knife and fork. Instead, using the bowl of her spoon for assistance if necessary, she twirls a manageable mouthful around the tines of her fork and transfers it to her mouth.

Pineapple: When a lady is served pineapple, it will most often be cut into rings or wedges, which she cuts into bite-sized pieces, using her fork (and her knife, if the fruit is tough). If the pineapple is served in its skin, however, she eats it in the same way she would eat a melon such as cantaloupe (see *Melon*).

Pizza: Pizza is one of the world's most informal, and potentially messy, foods. In most instances, in fact, a lady is expected to pick up an appealing slice and eat it using her fingers. If she finds that the pizza is still piping hot from the oven, and thus too hot to handle, or if it is loaded with messy, albeit tasty, toppings, she may wish to use a knife and fork. That decision, however, is entirely her own and is not dependent upon the behavior of anyone else at the table.

Quail and other small birds: A lady uses her knife and fork to slice off and eat as much meat as possible from the bird. Since some meat will inevitably remain on the bones, she may pick them up and tear away the tasty morsels with her teeth. She does so discreetly, however, avoiding any sucking noises.

Quesadillas: If the quesadilla is cooked in butter and is still warm and greasy, a lady eats it with her knife and fork. If it is served at room temperature and the grease is unlikely to ooze onto the table or her front, she may use her fingers to pick up a slice of the quesadilla. In either case, however, she keeps her napkin handy.

Sandwiches: In most cases, a lady eats a sandwich in the traditional way, using both hands. An open-faced sandwich or an extremely large, messy sandwich, such as a double-decker burger, may require that she resort to a knife and fork.

Shish kabob: To eat a shish kabob, a lady begins by picking up the skewer and using her dinner fork (not her fingers) to slide all the cubes of meat or vegetables onto her plate. She places the used skewer on the rim of her plate and uses her knife and fork to eat the meat and vegetables.

Steaks or chops: A lady uses her knife and fork to cut the meat into bite-sized pieces, cutting off one bite-sized morsel at a time. (She does not slice up the entire steak or chop before beginning to eat.) In the case of small, slender chops, such as the bone-in chops from rack of lamb, she does her best to cut the meat away from the bone, one bite at a time. Almost invariably, however, she will find that a good bit of meat will remain on the bone. At that point, she feels free to pick up the bone and tear away the meat, using her teeth, although she avoids making any unpleasant noises. A lady never picks up the bone from a sizable steak or chop.

Strawberries: If served on a plate or in a bowl, sliced and with the hulls removed, a lady eats strawberries with her fork or spoon. If served with the hull still attached, whether the berry is fresh from the garden or dipped in chocolate, a lady simply uses her fingers to remove the hull, discards it on her plate, and pops the berry into her mouth.

Sushi: When eating sushi, a lady may use either chopsticks or her fingers. If she does use her fingers, however, she makes sure to wash her hands thoroughly after the meal to eradicate any fishy smell.

To eat sushi with chopsticks:

1. Using the chopsticks, gently grip the sushi lengthwise, so the rice does not fall apart.

2. If you wish, gently dip the sushi, rice side down, in soy sauce or any other sauce that is provided.

3. Bring the sushi to your mouth. (Sushi is intended to be eaten in one or two bites, one bite after the other. A lady does not return half-eaten sushi to her plate.)

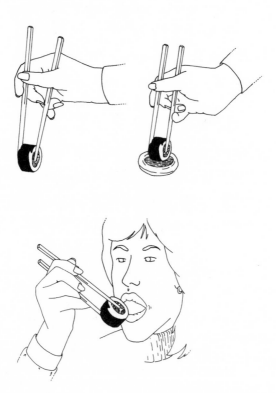

To eat sushi with your fingers, pick it up carefully, using your thumb and middle finger, then proceed as if you were using chopsticks.

A LADY TAKES THE LEAD

When a lady and her dining companions come to the table, she knows they may very well be looking to her for guidance, especially if she is the only lady at the table or if she is the hostess for the occasion. In such situations, the well-mannered gentlemen at the table will be waiting for her to begin her meal before they begin their own. If she is the hostess, even her lady guests will be waiting to follow her unspoken directions.

If she is hosting the meal and is occupied with actually getting the food on the table, she will be considerate enough to urge her guests to begin eating before their hot food gets cold or their cold food gets warm. When she tells them, "Please go ahead and begin," she means it and her guests are expected to comply with her wishes.

At the end of the meal, the guests will also be waiting to follow her lead. She makes it clear that the meal has ended by simply placing her casually folded napkin on the table beside her plate. If she wishes her guests to leave the table, she makes her wish clear, saying, "Why don't we move to the den [or the living room] for a drink [or for coffee]?"

3

Serving and Being Served

A Lady at a Private Dinner

A lady living alone may find it convenient to eat over the sink, or to eat from paper plates or whatever container her take-out comes in, but at times a lady will want to have friends or family over so that she can enjoy their company in her own home. Needless to say, she will find it much easier to rise to those occasions if she practices good table manners at every meal, even when *she* is the only person watching.

When she is hosting a meal for guests, a lady takes pains to be on her absolute best behavior. When she is seated at the head of her own table, she takes special care not to let her manners slip.

When a lady is entertaining
at home, she turns off the television,
unless the purpose of the party is to
watch a television program, such as a
ball game or a concert.

———

If a lady chooses to play
background music during a dinner
party, she makes sure it stays in
the background and does not
overwhelm the table conversation.

———

If a lady discovers that
she is running as much as fifteen
minutes late for a dinner party or for
cocktails, either in a private home or
in a restaurant, she makes every
attempt to contact her host or
hostess, urging that the party go
ahead without her.

———

Even if she is not a
praying person, when grace is
said or a prayer of blessing is offered
at any meal, a lady bows her head.
She need not feel compelled to
say "amen," however, unless
she wishes to do so.

––––

A lady never argues with
friends at the table.

––––

In the midst of a
dinner conversation—or any
conversation—a lady does not
attempt to make herself the
center of attention.

––––

A lady does not reach
or grab for food. Instead, she waits
for it to be passed by a fellow diner,
or served to her by a server.

––––

If a lady desires a second helping from any dish on the table, once everyone at the table has been served, she does not refrain from asking, "Would you please pass the dressing?" or "Might I have some more gravy?" or "I think I'd like a little more of the stroganoff. Would you please pass it my way?"

———

When it is a lady's turn to pass the breadbasket or a serving dish, she passes it around the table clockwise. (In other words, she passes it to her left.)

———

A lady does not wash down her food with great gulps of water, or any other beverage.

———

A lady does not salt her food before tasting it.

———

A lady does not "eat and run."

———

If a lady does not find an ashtray beside her place at the dinner table, she does not ask for one.

———

Unless she has been rudely served, in the extreme, a lady never corrects the behavior of a server at a private dinner party, as she understands that that person is the employee of her host or hostess.

———

As soon as her host or hostess shuts down the bar or turns off the coffeepot, a lady knows it is time to go home.

———

No matter how informal the event at which she has been entertained, a lady always says thank you, either in writing or by telephone.

———

A lady knows that the written thank-you note never goes out of style.

———

DINNER IS SERVED

If a lady attends even a few dinner parties, she will discover that her food may be served to her in a variety of ways. Almost all varieties of service, however, are based on one of three traditions.

English service: This service, also referred to as "family service," is the one most familiar to most ladies. The serving dishes are brought to the table by the host or hostess, and then passed from one guest to another. It is unnecessary for the host or hostess ever to leave the table, except to refill the water pitcher or breadbasket, or, if the serving dishes have been removed to a sideboard or returned to the kitchen, to offer second helpings of the main course or side dishes.

Russian service: This service, also known as "banquet service," is considerably more formal

than English service. In this system, servers
arrange the food on the plates and then set
them in front of the guests, or bring the
serving dishes around, allowing each guest to
serve himself or herself. Russian service, or a
version thereof, is the service provided at
almost all restaurants and at almost every
formal banquet, whether a fund-raiser or a
rehearsal dinner.

Mixed service: In this service, the main
course and its side dishes may be presented on
serving dishes at the table so that the guests
may serve themselves or be served by the host
or hostess. Soup, salad, and dessert, arranged
on individual plates, may be served directly
from the kitchen.

In any case, it is not a lady's responsibility to
define the manner in which her food is served
to her. Instead, she simply eats what is put in
front of her, as it is presented.

When a lady hosts a dinner party in her own home, however, it is her responsibility to decide how the meal will be served and to plan accordingly. She takes into account such factors as the formality of the evening, the size of her dining table (a small table may not be able to comfortably accommodate several serving dishes), and her desire to hire a server. Whatever choices she has made, a hostess serves dinner as follows:

- The hostess announces that dinner is ready and invites the guests to the table, showing them to their places.
- If she is serving a salad, the hostess places the salad plates directly on the dinner plates (which have already been set).
- When the guests have finished their salads, the hostess removes the salad plates. If she plans to serve the dinner plates in the kitchen, she takes them away at the same time. The salad forks are cleared away with the salad plates.

- The hostess either serves the dinner plates in the kitchen, or she brings the main course and its side dishes to the table, where the guests serve themselves.

- The hostess may wish to fill her guests' wine glasses for the first time herself. From then on, at an intimate gathering of friends, she encourages them to serve themselves, passing the bottle from person to person.

- When her guests have finished the main course, with second helpings if they are offered, the hostess clears away the dinner plates along with the dinner forks and knives.

- Salad may follow the entrée, if the hostess prefers.

- Finally, the hostess serves dessert. If she has not already placed the dessert forks or spoons on the table, she may bring them out along with the dessert itself. If there is coffee, she serves it now.

ON THE HOME VINE

When a lady entertains in her own home, she selects the wines that complement the dinner she is offering. She knows what she will be serving for the salad or fish course, so she chooses a wine that goes well with that course. To accompany her main course, she serves an appropriate wine of her own choosing, as if it were part of the entrée (which it is). If a guest is unhappy with the wine she has been served, and unless the lady has a considerable wine cellar, the host simply says to the guest, "I'm afraid that's the only suitable wine we have on hand. Would you prefer water or soda?"

Even if a lady maintains a fine wine cellar, she does not break into it simply to indulge the tastes of whimsical friends.

About Flowers and Candles

When a lady hosts a romantic dinner for two in her own home, fresh flowers and the soft glow of candles enhance her table. But the flowers need to be an asset to the table, not an obstruction. She arranges them in a low vase or bowl, so they don't prevent her from making eye contact with her guest. A lady shies away from overly aromatic blooms such as heavy-scented lilies, which can overpower even the strongest passion.

Candlelight makes anybody look more attractive, including the lady herself. As with flowers, candles should be positioned so that they are not an obstacle or a safety hazard. The lady lights them just before serving the salad course, and she makes sure to snuff them out before leaving the table. (When snuffing out candles, she cups one hand behind the flame, to prevent hot wax from spattering across the table and onto her guest.)

In order to make sure that her candles can be easily lit, a clever hostess tests them ahead of time, letting them burn for a few minutes so that some of the wax slides away from the wick.

Dining at Its Most Casual

Although a lady may occasionally be invited
to formal dinners, complete with white linen, a
panoply of flatware, and a steady parade of
dishes and wine glasses, she will more often be
included in at-home dinners of a much more
informal sort. These days, in fact, many homes
are designed with spacious dens or television
rooms or even kitchens that are large enough
for entertaining a medium-sized dinner party.

Even in the most casual of circumstances,
however, a lady does not forget her manners.
She makes careful use of her napkin, and she
attempts to avoid dropping her flatware or
spilling gravy on the floor, even if it is sealed in
stain-resistant polymers.

At parties such as this—whether the
occasion is a birthday, a holiday, or simply the
camaraderie of long-time friends—a lady may
have an opportunity to pitch in with the last-

minute preparation of the meal. She may be asked to toss the salad, to fill the water glasses, or to open the wine. At the end of the meal, she may even offer to help collect the dirty dishes, but she does not take it upon herself to provide assistance of any sort if her host or hostess has declined her offer. Only if she is an extremely intimate friend of the host or hostess—and only then if she is the last guest remaining—does she offer to help wash the dishes. No matter how good her intentions might be, a lady does not run the risk of embarrassing other guests, who may feel pressured to join in the cleanup party.

Once her host or hostess has said, "Thank you for the offer, Paige, but I'll just straighten these things up a little later," a lady does not force the issue. In this situation, as in every other situation, a lady knows how to take no for an answer.

TABLE TALK

When she is the host or a guest at any gathering, a lady does her best to make pleasant conversation, both for her own enjoyment and for the enjoyment of others. If she is among strangers or persons with whom she is not well acquainted, she always begins by introducing herself to the guest or guests standing or seated closest to her. If it seems necessary, she then introduces those guests to one another.

A lady may attempt to begin the conversation with the most innocuous of icebreakers, such as "Mary Jo certainly sets a lovely table, doesn't she?" or "Jim and Jack's garden really looks great this time of year, doesn't it?" In no case does she ask prying or personal questions. She may ask, "Are you from here in Topeka?" as that question allows her new friend to share as much personal information as he or she cares to divulge. She does not, however, begin the conversation by asking, "Now, just how is it that you know Mary Jo and Hiram?" (The guest, after all, may have been the doctor who cared for Hiram's recently deceased father, in which case the lady may find herself and her fellow guest involved in an unhappy topic.) Similarly, a lady does not open the conversation by asking, "And just what is it you do for a living, Madison?" as that question may imply that the lady considers her fellow guest's job to be the only thing interesting about his or her life. And in times of economic distress, it can be awkward for the guest who happens to be unhappily unemployed.

If a lady is seated next to a gentleman, she may open the conversation by paying him an unobtrusive compliment, such as "That's a very beautiful tie." She hopes, of course, that he will respond by saying something that will advance the conversation, such as, "Thank you. I bought it on my last visit to Spain" or "Thank you, I'm fond of it too."

A lady makes every effort to engage in conversation with both of the guests seated next to her. A long-standing rule of etiquette demands that she switch from one dinner partner to the other every time a new course is brought to the table. Such rigid obedience to rules is no longer expected or required: A lady need not break off an interesting discussion with the person on her right, or interrupt the conversation of the person on her left, simply because the salad course has arrived.

At a dinner table of any size, or in a crowded, noisy dining room, a lady does not attempt to engage the entire table in her conversation. Instead, she converses quietly with the people seated nearest to her. A lady never shouts at a dinner party.

Whether she is seated between strangers or next to her closest friends, a lady always steers away from potentially controversial subjects— which means that she avoids the topics of politics or religion at almost any cost. Should her dinner companion attempt to raise such topics, the lady does her best to change the subject. If she must do so, she simply says, "I'd prefer not to talk about that right now," and without letting the pace of the conversation lag, she proceeds by asking, "Have you seen the new Monica Maxwell movie? I think she's always a lot of fun."

FRAGILE—HANDLE WITH CARE

Even the most graceful, meticulous lady has her clumsy moments. While enjoying drinks before dinner, she may nudge a vase from an end table; during dinner, she may cause a wine goblet to slide off the table. She may send a cocktail glass shattering to the floor at any time.

In such cases, a lady's only immediate recourse is to say, "I'm sorry. May I help clean up?" Under no circumstances does a lady attempt to offer her host monetary compensation for the destroyed property. Instead, she attempts to replace it. (Of course, she does not attempt to replicate a family heirloom or find a substitute for a precious antique.) In any case, a lady sends her thank-you note for the party, including a reiteration of her apology, as soon as possible. Even in such situations, however, a lady does not grovel. She understands that, over the course of life, things get broken. She says "I'm sorry" as sincerely as possible. Then she moves on.

THE BUCK STOPS HERE

A lady does not offer to tip the bartenders or other servers at a private dinner party—even at a stand-up cocktail party where the lady's glass has been kept filled, repeatedly, by a watchful server. Neither does she attempt to tip the person who helps her with her hat and overcoat. Her assumption is that these helpful people will be paid and tipped at the end of the evening by her host or hostess.

The only exception to this rule is an occasion on which a lady has been offered some extraordinary kindness or unusual assistance. For example, a lady may need to ask a server for help if she discovers that the zipper of her dress has come loose, she loses a blouse button, or she finds herself feeling ill. In such circumstances she may rightfully offer the helpful server a few folded bills as an expression of her gratitude. She does this by simply passing the bills along to the friendly server, as part of a handshake. Especially in cases such as these, she never neglects to say thank you.

At some public events, such as charity fund-raisers—even those with an open bar—a lady may notice that the bartender has set up a "tip glass," with a few dollar bills already stuffed in to prime the pump. The tip glass may even be discreetly sequestered behind the bar, but not so discreetly that the lady does not see it. In such situations, a lady may choose to tip, or not to tip, as she pleases. If she expects to return to that bartender at any point in the evening, however, the lady will probably choose to tip, at least a dollar each time she visits the bar.

In all circumstances, a lady does, however, take it upon herself to tip valet parkers, if that service is provided. She tips the driver who brings her car around to her. At a party in a private home, a tip of two dollars will usually suffice. In a large city, especially at a restaurant, a lady may wish to tip as much as five dollars. If a lady only has a lone dollar bill in her purse, however, she pushes it into the valet's hand, slips behind the wheel of her car, and sails off into the night.

RESPONDING TO INVITATIONS

When she has been invited to dinner, a lady always responds promptly, whether she must accept or regret. If her plans change for an unforeseen and unavoidable reason, she again notifies her host or hostess as quickly as possible.

When she receives a dinner invitation from a married couple, a lady sends her acceptance or her regrets to her would-be hostess.

When a lady receives a dinner invitation
from an unmarried couple, she sends her
acceptance or her regrets to both of her would-
be hosts or hostesses. On the envelope she lists
their names in alphabetical order according to
their last names, and on the enclosed note of
acceptance or regrets she writes their first
names, also in alphabetical order.

If a lady has been entertained at dinner, she
always says thank you, either at the moment, by
phone the next day, or by a note, mailed within
the next forty-eight hours.

When a lady has been entertained by a
married couple, she sends her thank-you note
to her hostess. She may express her gratitude to
both her host and her hostess, but tradition
assumes that it is her hostess who has thrown
the party, and it is to the hostess that her
thank-you should be addressed.

When a lady has been entertained by an
unmarried couple, she follows the same procedure
with her thank-you note as with her response

note. She addresses it to both people, listing their names in alphabetical order by last name on the envelope, and their first names in alphabetical order on the enclosed thank-you note.

THE UNINVITED GUEST

If a lady has been brought to a party to which she has not specifically been invited and discovers that the party is a seated dinner with no room for her, she does not expect her host or hostess to set a place for her. Instead, she leaves immediately, realizing that there may not be enough food or flatware to accommodate her. It is not inappropriate for her to ask the friend who brought her to the party to drive her home. Or she may call a cab. In such circumstances she does the best she can to prevent inconveniencing or embarrassing the host or hostess. She exits as quickly and as graciously as possible, saying, "So sorry for the misunderstanding. I hope we can get together some time soon." In such situations, it is not the lady's responsibility to write a note of apology. That responsibility lies with the person who brought her, without warning, to the dinner.

4

IN THE PRESENCE OF OTHERS

DINING AT A RESTAURANT

Although many of the same rules apply as if she were dining in a private home—after all, a table is a table—when a lady is dining in a restaurant, some situations arise that are unique to that public world. Not only is she in the company of her own dinner partner (or partners), but she is also in a room surrounded by many other diners, each of whom is hoping to enjoy a pleasant meal. However, a lady need not be intimidated by such situations, no matter how elegant the décor or the clientele. From choosing wine to pronouncing an unfamiliar word on a menu, a lady can learn how to maneuver in a restaurant, enabling her to start out the evening with an advantage.

Unless her host or hostess
lights up first, or she is in the
absolute privacy of her own home
or in the smoking section of a
restaurant, a lady never smokes
at the table.

————

If a lady feels that
she must light up a cigarette in
a restaurant and her table is in
the no-smoking section, she
heads for the bar.

————

Whenever a lady
heads out for a night on
the town, whether as the hostess
or a guest for the evening, she makes
sure to carry a supply of dollar
bills so that she is ready to tip
valet parkers, doormen, and
washroom attendants whenever
the need arises.

————

A Lady at the Table

In a restaurant, if a lady
wants a steak knife, she asks for
one, saying "Thank you very much"
when it has been provided.

––––

A lady assumes that her food
will be served to her from the left,
and that her empty dishes will be
cleared away from the right.

––––

If a lady is asked to offer a
toast—or if she chooses to offer
one, of her own accord—she keeps
it brief, tasteful, and to the point.

––––

A lady says please and thank
you, especially to servers—either
in a restaurant or in a private home.

––––

When she is expected to
pay for her own meal in a restaurant,
a lady is not ashamed to ask the
price of any special item
offered by the server.

––––

If another diner asks to sample
a lady's food and the lady is willing
to oblige, she may respond by asking
her fellow diner to lend the lady his
or her fork and bread plate, so the
lady can offer a small portion
of the requested dish.

———

If a lady truly finds it
unpleasant or awkward to share
her food with others, she simply
declines the request, saying,
"Everybody's food looks so delicious.
Let's just stick to our own plates, if
you don't mind."

———

For her own part, however,
under no circumstances does a lady
ask to taste another person's food.

———

When dining in a restaurant,
a lady feels free to ask for a
"doggie bag" or a "to-go box."

———

Should the diners at a table
close to her own become so
boisterous as to imperil the pleasure
of the lady's own dinner companions,
she does not attempt to chasten
them. Instead, she leaves her table to
seek the assistance of the maître d',
the host, or the hostess.

If a lady knows the first name
of any server in a restaurant,
she feels free to use it.

GATHERINGS IN RESTAURANTS

More and more often, when it comes to entertaining, a lady finds herself at a restaurant, whether she is the host or a guest. The occasion may be a business meal, a simple gathering of friends, or the celebration of a birthday, an anniversary, or some other milestone.

No matter what the reason for the dinner, a lady knows that her behavior in a public place may be scrutinized even more closely than at a private party.

The Lady as Hostess

When a lady intends to host a dinner for friends at a restaurant, she always makes it clear whether she is paying the entire bill or whether each person is expected to pay his or her share. She may say, "I hope you and Jenny will be my guests for dinner at the Gewgaw Club on Saturday night." Alternatively, if the lady merely intends to bring together a group of friends, each of whom is expected to pay his or her own way for the evening, she may say, "I was wondering if you and Paolo would be available for dinner on Friday night. I was thinking we'd stop in at Loco Coco, around eight—very casual, dutch treat."

If the lady's invitation is accepted, she makes sure that her guests know the time of the dinner reservation, the address and phone number of the restaurant, and any dress code that is required for the gentlemen in the party. Fewer and fewer restaurants require that a gentleman wear a coat and tie, even for dinner, but such requirements do persist in some establishments, and a hostess is always wise to ask ahead of time rather than risk embarrassing one of her guests. If there is a dress code for gentlemen, it may also give her lady guests some indication as to how they may choose to dress for the evening.

In choosing a restaurant at which to entertain her friends or business clients, a lady does her best to select an establishment where everyone at the table can make a happy choice from the menu. In most restaurants nowadays, the menu includes at least one vegetarian selection, but a lady takes extra precautions before inviting her friends to an ethnic restaurant or one that is noted for its unusual cuisine. Her best course is to be straightforward, saying, "A group of us are going to that wonderful Thai restaurant on Mobberly Road." If her guest is not fond of Thai cuisine, the lady may elect to suggest another restaurant. If the hostess has made it clear that a group of friends are involved in the party, the well-mannered invitee who does not enjoy Thai food will say, "I think I'll take a pass this time. Thai doesn't settle well with me. I hope you'll give me a rain check."

If several other friends have already accepted the lady's invitation, it will be difficult for her to rearrange the entire excursion, although she may be willing to go beyond the call of duty to do so. Meanwhile, if the Thai-negative friend is the first to be asked, the hostess will find it easy to adjust her plans. In either case, once the hostess has revamped the evening to accommodate the guest's preferences, the guest must accept the invitation and do her best to be a glad participant in the dinner party.

A lady does her best to arrive at the restaurant ahead of, or at least along with, her guests so that she can claim the reservation and make sure her guests are not left lingering in the foyer or at the bar. If there is a delay before her party is seated, her guests may choose to have a drink at the bar. If she is paying for the entire dinner, the hostess picks up the bar tab, as well, leaving an appropriate tip for the bartender. It is not bad form for a guest to offer to pay for a round of drinks. A hostess may accept or decline the offer, as she chooses.

When her party's table is ready, the hostess may choose to dictate who sits next to whom. If the occasion is purely social, she seats her guests as she would seat them in her own home.

If the occasion is a business meal, she seats her guests in an arrangement that expedites the work to be done.

In most restaurants a server will appear, almost immediately, to fill the party's water glasses and ask if anybody would like anything else to drink. The guests may, of course, order anything they please, whether it is a cocktail, wine or beer, iced tea, or a soda. When the server returns with the drinks, he or she may inform the party of any "specials" available that evening that are not included on the printed menu. If the guests have questions, they ask them, particularly if they are concerned about food allergies or carbohydrate intake. Any guest may simply ask, "Does the spinach salad have nuts in it?" or "Is it possible for me to get the Sunrise Pasta without the shrimp?"

The server may recommend appetizers, but they need not be ordered if the diners have no interest in them. The hostess may choose to tell the waiter, "We'd like a few minutes, please." All the guests then turn their focus to the menu so they can be ready to order when the server returns. The hostess does not hurry her guests along; the guests themselves, however, do their best to keep the dinner running on a smooth schedule.

If the lady wants to steer her friends away from the more expensive cuisine, she may suggest, "I understand the grilled salmon is delicious." (However, a lady always checks out the prices at any restaurant before she invites friends or clients to dine there on her tab.) If a guest chooses instead to order the filet mignon, the hostess does not flinch.

After all her guests have finished their entrées, desserts, after-dinner drinks, and coffee, a lady may ask for the bill. Her guests may offer to pitch in to help pay the tab, but if she invited them as guests, she simply says, "No, thank you. You're my guests for the evening."

Once the lady has made it clear, ahead of time, that everybody is to pay his or her own way, she requests in advance that the server provide separate checks. (At a party where nobody is clearly the "host," it is appropriate for anybody at the table to request separate checks.) If the restaurant has a no-separate-checks policy, and if everybody's bill seems to be approximately the same, and if all her fellow diners approve, she may ask the server simply to split the bill equally among the guests, or among the couples, as the case may be.

A lady does her best to make sure her guests know that the party is going dutch. Unless she is already familiar with the restaurant, she calls ahead to ask if separate checks are offered. If she is told that the restaurant has a no-separate-checks policy, she passes that information along to the other people in her group, so that they can bring along cash to pitch in when it comes time for the lady to coordinate the payment of the bill. (And, if she has extended the invitation, it will be her responsibility to make sure the bill has been paid, with an appropriate tip added in, at the end of the evening, although it may require her asking, "Does anybody have a couple more dollars for the tip?") Even without requesting a separate check, a guest may attempt to pay her portion of the bill with a credit card, simply asking, "Would you please put fifty dollars on this card?" Nevertheless, some restaurants refuse to make even this concession.

In such situations, the hostess is faced with the challenge of being fair to everyone at the table, but she also does her best to be fair to herself, in hopes that she will not be left paying an inordinate share of the bill. She may decree, "It looks like everybody's share, tip included, is fifty dollars." Or she may take the risk of suggesting, "Everybody pitch in whatever seems right." The latter option certainly demonstrates consideration for the guest who only drank iced tea and ordered the chicken sandwich, but it also leaves the lady vulnerable to the undependable generosity and sobriety, or even the honesty, of her fellow guests. She may be wiser to propose, "Each person's share is fifty dollars. Is that OK with everybody?" Given that option, the guest who's eaten modestly has every right to say, "If it's all right with you, I believe my share is more like twenty dollars." It is the guest's responsibility to contribute a fair share of the bill, remembering to cover his or her share of the tip. It is the lady's responsibility to say, "Sure, Gus. That sounds fine."

If there is only one check, it is the lady's responsibility to determine the server's tip and to include it in the shared total for the evening. If a tip for the wine steward or the maître d' is requested, the lady includes it in the shared total.

The Lady as Guest

If a lady is invited for dinner in a restaurant, either as a friend or a business colleague, she accepts or declines the invitation as soon as possible. If the invitation is to a restaurant where she knows she does not like or cannot eat the food, she states that fact clearly. Without further elaboration, she says, "You're kind to invite me, Barbara, but the menu at Middle Europa doesn't work very well for me." If the intent of the luncheon or the dinner is to do business, and if the lady's opinion is asked, she says, "Middle Europa doesn't work well for me. Can we choose some other place?"

If a lady is fortunate, the friend who invited her to dinner will have made her intentions as clear as possible regarding who is paying the bill. The thoughtful hostess will have avoided any confusion by saying either, "I hope you'll be my guest next Friday evening at the Rossland House," or "Are you available for dinner at the Rossland House next Friday? It'll be dutch treat. I think we'll have a good time."

If the lady knows that the Rossland House is beyond her price range and the dinner is to be dutch treat (or if the hostess has left her uncertain as to who will pay), the lady simply says, "Thanks so much, Barbara, but I'm afraid I already have an engagement for Friday night. I wish I could join you, but maybe we can grab a drink sometime soon." This is as much explanation as a lady need offer when declining any invitation. If a lady's wallet decrees that she cannot afford to accept Barbara's invitation, her safest course is to stay home or to bring together a group of other friends for an evening of burgers and fries at a more moderately priced restaurant. All the while, she remains fully confident that, before long, the Rossland House will be within her budget. She does not overextend herself now, however, simply to keep up with more affluent friends.

If a lady accepts an invitation, she does her best to help make the evening a success. If she and other diners have enjoyed drinks at the bar before they are seated at their table, she may offer to pay the bar tab. In no case does she argue with her host, however. She may say, "Please, let me do this," but if the host declines the offer, she drops the issue.

When it comes to ordering her dinner, if separate checks are not available, she attempts to order in the same price range as her fellow diners to avoid inequities when the check is split at the end of the evening. In such situations, if everybody else is ordering fish or chicken, she does not order steak.

If a lady has eaten less expensively than others in the party, she offers to pay her fair share (a lady does not forget to include a tip) when it comes time to divide the bill. Again, if a lady feels awkward about speaking up on her own behalf, and if she knows that her fellow diners are big spenders, she does not diminish her enjoyment of the evening by worrying about how much she will have to pay. If such are her fears, she declines the invitation.

If the host has ordered wine for the table, and if the lady is a teetotaler, and if it is not an assault on her personal morality, she may still choose to pay an equal share of the bill. The cost of fine wine can be prohibitive, however, and the nondrinking lady need not feel obliged to help in paying for it. When it comes time to pay the bill, she contributes her fair share. She does not say, "Martha, you know I'm not a drinker, so I'm not going to pay for any of that."

At all times throughout a restaurant dinner, a lady attempts to maintain a congenial, businesslike relationship with her server. If she is a guest at the table, and if she feels she is being rudely or ineptly served, she informs her host of that fact, saying, "Horace, I'm really having a problem with this server. He and I simply aren't getting along. Would you mind checking in with the manager?"

COUPON ETIQUETTE

When a lady is dining at a restaurant and has a coupon for a discounted meal or a free drink, dessert, or other item, she offers the coupon to her server before she and her fellow diners have begun to order their meal. The server may say, "I'll take the coupon at the end of the meal," but at least he will know to ask for it before totaling the bill. A lady does not assume that she will be given inferior service simply because she has offered a discount coupon to pay for part of her meal.

If a lady makes use of a discount coupon, or if she has been offered a complimentary item, such as a drink, an appetizer, or a dessert, she leaves her server the same tip she would have provided if she were paying full price. She knows that her bill will usually indicate the pre-discount price of the meal. If she must consult a menu to determine the price of the complimentary item, she does so.

Dining at the Bar

From time to time, in a restaurant of virtually any type, a lady may choose to take her luncheon or dinner at the bar. She need not drink alcohol to do so. Her only assumption—and the only assumption of the bartender—is that she wishes to dine efficiently, with attentive service.

Whether or not she drinks alcohol, a lady may establish a congenial relationship with the man or woman behind the bar. The bartender's job is not to push liquor upon customers (the law proscribes this). His or her job is simply to provide congenial, bartenderly service.

If she is an inveterate bar diner, a lady may be skilled in striking up conversations—either with the bartender or with other patrons. She is careful at all times, however, not to distract the bartender from his or her job. And, unless a ready opportunity seems to be provided, she is especially careful not to intrude upon the conversations of fellow bar-goers. If she attempts to strike up a conversation with another customer at the bar, and if her fellow customer clearly prefers to dine or drink in peace, a lady respects those wishes.

If she has enjoyed her entire dinner at the bar (even if her drink consisted of nothing more than iced tea), when it comes time for tipping, a lady remembers the personal attention she has been shown, tipping a minimum of 15 percent for acceptable service, and 20 percent if the bartender has been particularly attentive. It is the lady's responsibility to be kind to the bartender when she leaves the place. If she forgets this sort of attention, she should not be surprised that it takes her a great deal longer to get her iced tea the next time she comes to the bar.

THE WELL-FILLED GLASS

If she is hosting a dinner party in a fine restaurant, a lady will probably be presented with a wine list. If the lady is a connoisseur of wines, she may select them for the entire table. If she is not confident of her own knowledge of wines, she may ask another diner to make the selections. If she is serving as host—and especially if she is paying the bill—she asks that guest to select "something in the $30 to $50 range," or the "$50 to $90 range," whichever she can afford. Even if wine has been ordered by the bottle, she encourages friends to order a glass of any wine they prefer—although wine, by the glass, generally costs considerably more than wine, per glass, from a bottle.

The age-old truism is that white wines go best with chicken or fish, moderately hearty red wines such as Pinot Noir and Zinfandel taste best with pork and lamb, and heavy, spicy reds, such as Cabernet and Shiraz, hold up best against beef. But such rules mean nothing nowadays, when a tuna steak may be every bit as rich as a filet of beef—or when a heavy steak may seem to require something dry, if that's what the diner desires. In short, the hostess may not be able to find a bottle of wine, or even two bottles of wine, to satisfy the whole table. She may have to pay for individual glasses of wine—and hence have to pay a great deal more when it comes time to pay the bill.

When the bottle of wine is brought to the table, it will be presented to the gentleman or lady who ordered it—whether or not that person is the host. (If the wine is presented to the hostess, and she did not select it, she asks the server to present it to the guest who selected it.) In any case, somebody must inspect the label on the wine bottle to make sure the wine is actually the wine that was ordered.

When the server (in a fine restaurant it will be the wine steward, or *sommelier*), brings the wine to the table, it will be uncorked in the presence of the hostess or whoever selected it. The server will then offer the cork to the person who selected the wine. The intent of this ritual is not to allow the guest to sniff the cork, to see whether it smells appetizing.

Instead, the guest is expected to test the cork, squeezing it lightly to see if it is dried out. If the cork feels dry, the tester may expect the wine to taste inordinately acidic and may request an alternative selection.

White wines may be opened close to the time they are to be served, and should be kept cold but not chilled. Red wines, however, should be ordered as soon as it has been determined that red wine will be desired by any of the diners. This is so the bottles can be opened and allowed to "breathe" before they are served.

How to Make a Toast

Over the course of her life, a lady will probably be invited to any number of wedding receptions, anniversary dinners, birthday parties, and other events. At some time, almost inevitably, she will be asked to make a toast, and if she is asked, she must not refuse. However, she need not attempt to give an after-dinner speech or perform a comedy routine. Her tribute may be something as simple as "Joe, I'm proud to call you my friend." She may choose to share some memory of her friendship with the honoree, or if she is confident of her skill as a humorist, she may toss off a lighthearted quip. In no case does she attempt to embarrass the guest of honor. Neither does she ramble on at any length. A lady remembers that because toasts usually come late in the evening, the wisest course is always to be succinct.

A Fair Percentage

When she serves as hostess in a restaurant, a lady understands that she is responsible for tipping any servers and other staff members who have assisted her party during the luncheon or dinner.

Whether she is paying in cash, on a company account, or with a credit card, a lady understands that the minimum standard for a tip—assuming that the table server has provided even acceptable service—is 15 percent of the bill, before tax. A tip of 20 percent is expected for service that is even remotely superior. If a lady finds her service to be extraordinary, or even particularly gracious, she may tip even more generously.

In any restaurant, a lady may not assume that servers are salaried employees. In many instances, the largest portion of their income comes from their tips, and in many fine restaurants, servers will be expected to share those tips with the busboys, bartenders, and others who help at the lady's table. If she has been served well, she does her best to tip fairly.

In many instances at restaurants, when the lady is hosting a large party (eight to ten persons or more) the establishment will add a gratuity to the bill. (Eighteen percent is the percentage often added to the total in restaurants nowadays.) A lady will find this detail in small print on the menu, and perhaps on the bill as well. (It behooves a lady to look closely and use her reading glasses if required—otherwise she may find herself tipping an additional 20 percent on top of the 18 percent already added on.) A lady may find this built-in percentage sufficient, or she may wish to add an additional gratuity. (Her credit card slip will probably offer her the opportunity to do so, or she may leave additional cash.)

In especially fine restaurants with respectable wine cellars, a lady may discover that the bill suggests that she provide a tip for the wine steward, or *sommelier*. If such is the case, and— once again, if the service has been acceptable— a lady adds a tip of 15 to 20 percent of the cost of the wine only, in gratitude for the wine steward's help.

The lady may choose to pay her bill, or leave her tip, in cash. (Many servers prefer cash tips, because cash payment means they do not have to wait for credit card charges to clear the bank.) If she is dining in a fine restaurant with a wine steward, and if she is tipping in cash, a lady does not forget to tip the wine steward, and the host of the restaurant, on her way out the door.

In most instances, as the lady is exiting, the host or maître d' will approach her with outstretched hand, saying, "I hope you had a lovely evening." If the lady expects to receive good service in that restaurant again, she is prepared to shake hands with each of them, slipping a twenty-dollar bill into the handshake. If she has already added a generous tip to her credit card bill, she feels no need to add this extra kindness. Both the steward and the host will be aware of, and will share in, her generosity when the credit card tips are apportioned and sorted out at the end of the evening.

At mid-range restaurants, the sort where most ladies dine, such concerns are irrelevant. In most cases the lady must simply decide how much she wants to leave for her server, with the server deciding how to split the cash gratuities among the other staff members at the close of the evening.

Under no circumstances is a lady intimidated into overtipping for poor service. She understands that some problems, such as slow service from the bar or the kitchen, are not the table server's fault. If she feels she has been served in a slovenly manner, however, she does not insult her own reputation by leaving a tip of five cents, twenty-five cents, or even five dollars on a sizeable tab. Instead, she leaves nothing at all, but before she leaves the restaurant, she finds the manager or host and explains the reasons for her decision.

Whatever the size of her tip, a lady offers it discreetly. After she has added the tip to her credit card slip, she turns it over and either encloses it in the bill cover provided by the restaurant or hands it directly to the server. Under no circumstance does a lady brag about or grouse about the size of her tip.

When a lady has ordered drinks at the bar before dinner, even if the bartender offers to transfer the bar bill to the lady's table, she leaves a gratuity for the bartender as her party moves to its table.

If she visits the bathroom and discovers an attendant there, even if that attendant offers her no particular service, a lady is expected to drop a dollar into the attendant's tip basket. She does so each time she stops by the ladies' room, for whatever reason. The attendant's job is to make sure the ladies' room is kept clean and well stocked with paper towels and bath tissue. A lady should not expect to see such an attendant very often, because even in the largest cities, ladies' room attendants are infrequently employed, except by upscale restaurants.

When tipping in cash, a lady never leaves loose change, unless it is a sizable pocketful of loose change. These days, a tip of less than one dollar is considered no tip at all.

If a lady dines at a diner, a breakfast bar, or any other establishment where customers are expected to pay at the cash register, she leaves her tip on the table before heading for the cashier. If she does not have the appropriate amount of cash in her purse at that moment, she asks for change at the cash register, returning to the table, tip in hand, as quickly as possible after paying her bill. If a lady uses a credit card to pay her bill at the cash register, she makes sure to add in a tip for her server, just as if she were filling out the credit card slip at the table.

Upon departing the restaurant, a lady is prepared to provide the valet parkers with a minimum tip of two dollars—or as much as five dollars, depending on the formality of the restaurant. If a lady has only one dollar in her purse at that late point in the evening, she does not apologize. Instead, she pushes the dollar bill into the parker's hand, saying, "Have a nice evening." A lady tries to plan ahead for all eventualities, but occasionally she may have no other option.

ON THE MENU

Nothing can show more quickly that a lady is out of her element than ordering an item off a menu and mispronouncing it—or, worse yet, having it arrive at the table and then realizing that she has just ordered something she does not enjoy or simply cannot eat. These days, a lady may find menus filled with items that never turned up on her mother's table. The following list may help a lady avoid awkward moments.

WHAT IT SAYS: **al dente**
WHAT IT MEANS: cooked but still firm—not mushy; usually refers to pasta or rice
HOW YOU PRONOUNCE IT: al dent tay

WHAT IT SAYS: **Alfredo**
WHAT IT MEANS: a cream-based sauce served with pasta
HOW YOU PRONOUNCE IT: al fray doh

WHAT IT SAYS: **arugula**
WHAT IT MEANS: a member of the mustard greens family, used primarily in salads
HOW YOU PRONOUNCE IT: ah roo guh lah

WHAT IT SAYS: **Asiago**

WHAT IT MEANS: a hard, pale yellow cheese, usually grated

HOW YOU PRONOUNCE IT: ah zhe ah go

WHAT IT SAYS: **au gratin**

WHAT IT MEANS: covered with bread crumbs or cheese and browned under a broiler

HOW YOU PRONOUNCE IT: oh grah ten

WHAT IT SAYS: **au jus**

WHAT IT MEANS: a method of serving broiled or grilled meat in its natural juices

HOW YOU PRONOUNCE IT: oh zhoo

WHAT IT SAYS: **balsamic vinegar**

WHAT IT MEANS: an aged vinegar made from white grapes, manufactured exclusively in Modena, Italy

HOW YOU PRONOUNCE IT: bal sah mick

WHAT IT SAYS: **basmati**

WHAT IT MEANS: a long-grained brown or white rice

HOW YOU PRONOUNCE IT: bahs mah tee

WHAT IT SAYS: **béarnaise**

WHAT IT MEANS: a smooth-textured sauce made of butter, eggs, shallots, white wine, and vinegar or lemon juice

HOW YOU PRONOUNCE IT: behr nayz

WHAT IT SAYS: **beurre blanc**

WHAT IT MEANS: a hot butter sauce flavored with vinegar or lemon

HOW YOU PRONOUNCE IT: burr blahnk

WHAT IT SAYS: **biscotti**

WHAT IT MEANS: a twice-baked Italian cookie, usually flavored with almonds or anise

HOW YOU PRONOUNCE IT: bee skawt tee

WHAT IT SAYS: **bisque**

WHAT IT MEANS: a thick cream soup often featuring shellfish or a vegetable, such as tomatoes

HOW YOU PRONOUNCE IT: bisk

WHAT IT SAYS: **bleu cheese**

WHAT IT MEANS: a sharp-flavored whitish cheese veined with

blue mold (which gives the cheese its distinctive tang)

How you pronounce it: blue cheese

What it says: **bolognese**

What it means: a style of serving pasta in a sauce made with tomatoes and ground meat

How you pronounce it: bowl ah naze

What it says: **brioche**

What it means: a sweet French bread made with eggs and butter

How you pronounce it: bree ohsh

What it says: **bruschetta**

What it means: toasted Italian bread, drizzled with olive oil, frequently topped with garlic and tomatoes

How you pronounce it: broo skeh tah

What it says: **cacciatore**

What it means: a style of slowly cooking meat or chicken along with tomatoes, herbs, and sometimes wine

How you pronounce it: kah chuh tor ee

WHAT IT SAYS: **café au lait**

WHAT IT MEANS: strong coffee, mixed in equal parts with steaming hot milk

HOW YOU PRONOUNCE IT: kafay oh lay

WHAT IT SAYS: **calamari**

WHAT IT MEANS: squid

HOW YOU PRONOUNCE IT: kal uh mahr ee

WHAT IT SAYS: **canapé**

WHAT IT MEANS: an hors d'oevure, such as a pâté or other spread, served on a cracker or toast

HOW YOU PRONOUNCE IT: can uh pee

WHAT IT SAYS: **carpaccio**

WHAT IT MEANS: ground or thinly sliced raw meat or fish, served with a sauce

HOW YOU PRONOUNCE IT: kahr pah chee oh

WHAT IT SAYS: **chanterelle**

WHAT IT MEANS: an edible, trumpet-shaped mushroom

HOW YOU PRONOUNCE IT: shan tuh rehl

WHAT IT SAYS: **chipotle**

WHAT IT MEANS: a red chili pepper used in Mexican cuisine

HOW YOU PRONOUNCE IT: chih poht lay

WHAT IT SAYS: **consommé**

WHAT IT MEANS: clear soup made from a well-seasoned beef
or chicken stock

HOW YOU PRONOUNCE IT: kon suh may

WHAT IT SAYS: **cordon bleu**

WHAT IT MEANS: a style of serving meat, usually veal or
chicken, by rolling it around slices of ham and cheese and
coating it in bread crumbs

HOW YOU PRONOUNCE IT: kor dohn bluh

WHAT IT SAYS: **coulis**

WHAT IT MEANS: a simple sauce made with puréed
vegetables or fruit

HOW YOU PRONOUNCE IT: koo lee

WHAT IT SAYS: **couscous**

WHAT IT MEANS: a tiny grain-sized pasta, frequently used in Mediterranean cuisine

HOW YOU PRONOUNCE IT: koos koos

WHAT IT SAYS: **crème brûlée**

WHAT IT MEANS: a custard sprinkled with sugar and then broiled so that the sugar forms a hard-candy topping

HOW YOU PRONOUNCE IT: krehm broo lay

WHAT IT SAYS: **crème caramel**

WHAT IT MEANS: a baked custard topped with caramel

HOW YOU PRONOUNCE IT: krehm kehr ah mehl

WHAT IT SAYS: **crepe**

WHAT IT MEANS: a paper-thin pancake

HOW YOU PRONOUNCE IT: krayp

WHAT IT SAYS: **crepes suzette**

WHAT IT MEANS: crepes warmed in an orange butter sauce and often presented dramatically in a blaze of flaming liquor

HOW YOU PRONOUNCE IT: krayp soo zeht

WHAT IT SAYS: **demi-glace**

WHAT IT MEANS: a concentrated beef-based sauce lightened with consommé

HOW YOU PRONOUNCE IT: dehm ee glahs

WHAT IT SAYS: **demitasse**

WHAT IT MEANS: a small cup of very strong coffee, usually served at the end of a dinner party

HOW YOU PRONOUNCE IT: dehm ee tahss

WHAT IT SAYS: **escargot**

WHAT IT MEANS: edible snails, usually sautéed in butter, sometimes served in their own shells

HOW YOU PRONOUNCE IT: ehs kahr goh

WHAT IT SAYS: **fennel**

WHAT IT MEANS: a licorice-flavored vegetable served either raw in a salad, or as a cooked side dish

HOW YOU PRONOUNCE IT: fehn uhl

WHAT IT SAYS: **feta**

WHAT IT MEANS: a classic Greek curd cheese made with sheep's or goat's milk

HOW YOU PRONOUNCE IT: feht uh

WHAT IT SAYS: **fettuccine**

WHAT IT MEANS: a flat pasta cut into long, thin strips

HOW YOU PRONOUNCE IT: feht tuh chee neh

WHAT IT SAYS: **flan**

WHAT IT MEANS: a simple egg custard, coated with caramel syrup, identical to crème caramel (see *crème caramel*)

HOW YOU PRONOUNCE IT: flahn

WHAT IT SAYS: **focaccia**

WHAT IT MEANS: a flat Italian bread seasoned with herbs and olive oil

HOW YOU PRONOUNCE IT: foe kah chyah

WHAT IT SAYS: **foie gras**

WHAT IT MEANS: the liver of a goose, enriched by force-feeding the bird a diet of rich grains

HOW YOU PRONOUNCE IT: fwah grah

WHAT IT SAYS: **frittata**

WHAT IT MEANS: an unfolded omelet featuring meat and/or vegetables

HOW YOU PRONOUNCE IT: frih tah tuh

WHAT IT SAYS: **ganache**

WHAT IT MEANS: a sweet, creamy chocolate mixture used as a filling or frosting

HOW YOU PRONOUNCE IT: gahn ahsh

WHAT IT SAYS: **génoise**

WHAT IT MEANS: a sponge cake made of butter and stiffly beaten eggs

HOW YOU PRONOUNCE IT: zhayn wahz

WHAT IT SAYS: **gnocchi**

WHAT IT MEANS: a small dumpling made of ground potatoes, broiled or baked, and served with a sauce or grated cheese

HOW YOU PRONOUNCE IT: noh kee

WHAT IT SAYS: **granita**

WHAT IT MEANS: a coarse-textured frozen dessert, usually made with fruit

HOW YOU PRONOUNCE IT: grah nee tah

WHAT IT SAYS: **hollandaise**

WHAT IT MEANS: a sauce made from butter, eggs, and lemon juice

HOW YOU PRONOUNCE IT: hol uhn dayz

WHAT IT SAYS: **hors d'oeuvre**

WHAT IT MEANS: light snacks served at cocktail parties or before a meal

HOW YOU PRONOUNCE IT: or derv

WHAT IT SAYS: **jalapeño**

WHAT IT MEANS: a hot green or red pepper

HOW YOU PRONOUNCE IT: hah lah peh nyoh

WHAT IT SAYS: **Kiev**

WHAT IT MEANS: a classic method of cooking chicken breasts, stuffed with herbs and garlic butter

HOW YOU PRONOUNCE IT: kee ehv

WHAT IT SAYS: **latte**

WHAT IT MEANS: a strong espresso coffee topped with frothy steamed milk

HOW YOU PRONOUNCE IT: lah tay

WHAT IT SAYS: **linguine**

WHAT IT MEANS: a flat pasta cut into long slender strips

HOW YOU PRONOUNCE IT: lihn gwee nee

WHAT IT SAYS: **lyonnaise**

WHAT IT MEANS: a style of seasoning food, using onions and parsley

HOW YOU PRONOUNCE IT: lee uh nayz

WHAT IT SAYS: **marsala**

WHAT IT MEANS: a sweet Italian wine often used to flavor chicken or veal

HOW YOU PRONOUNCE IT: mahr sah lah

WHAT IT SAYS: **Mornay**

WHAT IT MEANS: a thick, velvety cheese sauce

HOW YOU PRONOUNCE IT: mohr nay

WHAT IT SAYS: **mousse**

WHAT IT MEANS: either a frothy chilled dessert, or a light, foamy seafood dish, served cold

HOW YOU PRONOUNCE IT: moose

WHAT IT SAYS: **mousseline**

WHAT IT MEANS: a smooth-textured, delicate sauce to which whipped cream or egg whites have been added

HOW YOU PRONOUNCE IT: moose leen

WHAT IT SAYS: **mussel**

WHAT IT MEANS: a marine or freshwater mollusk, usually steamed with wine

HOW YOU PRONOUNCE IT: muss uhl

WHAT IT SAYS: **niçoise**

WHAT IT MEANS: a style of serving cold vegetables or seafood with tomatoes and olive oil, often including black olives and garlic

HOW YOU PRONOUNCE IT: nee swahz

WHAT IT SAYS: **osso buco**

WHAT IT MEANS: a sliced veal knuckle or shinbone, slow-cooked in olive oil and wine

HOW YOU PRONOUNCE IT: aw soh boo koh

WHAT IT SAYS: **paella**

WHAT IT MEANS: a dish of shellfish, chicken, and rice,

flavored with saffron

HOW YOU PRONOUNCE IT: pie ay yuh

WHAT IT SAYS: **pancetta**

WHAT IT MEANS: lean, unsmoked bacon used in Italian

cuisine, similar to Canadian bacon

HOW YOU PRONOUNCE IT: pan cheh tuh

WHAT IT SAYS: **panini**

WHAT IT MEANS: a grilled sandwich of vegetables, cheese,

and sometimes meat, served in focaccia (see *focaccia*)

HOW YOU PRONOUNCE IT: pah nee nee

WHAT IT SAYS: **Parmesan**

WHAT IT MEANS: a dry-textured, sharp-flavored Italian

cheese, often grated

HOW YOU PRONOUNCE IT: pahr muh zahn

WHAT IT SAYS: **pâté**

WHAT IT MEANS: meat or fowl, finely minced or ground, seasoned and chilled in a loaf-shaped mold

HOW YOU PRONOUNCE IT: pah tay

WHAT IT SAYS: **penne**

WHAT IT MEANS: pasta cut on the diagonal into short tubes

HOW YOU PRONOUNCE IT: pen nay

WHAT IT SAYS: **pesto**

WHAT IT MEANS: an Italian sauce made of basil, garlic, pine nuts, olive oil, and grated cheese

HOW YOU PRONOUNCE IT: peh stoh

WHAT IT SAYS: **phyllo**

WHAT IT MEANS: tissue-thin sheets of pastry, used most often in Greek dishes

HOW YOU PRONOUNCE IT: fee loh

WHAT IT SAYS: **piccata**

WHAT IT MEANS: a style of serving thinly pounded cutlets of meat or chicken, sautéed in lemon and butter

HOW YOU PRONOUNCE IT: pih kah tuh

WHAT IT SAYS: **pilaf**

WHAT IT MEANS: a dish consisting of seasoned rice or grains mixed with onions, raisins, lentils or other legumes, dried fruits, or vegetables

HOW YOU PRONOUNCE IT: pee lahf

WHAT IT SAYS: **pistou**

WHAT IT MEANS: a sauce made of basil, garlic, and olive oil

HOW YOU PRONOUNCE IT: pees too

WHAT IT SAYS: **polenta**

WHAT IT MEANS: a thick mush made of cornmeal boiled in stock or water

HOW YOU PRONOUNCE IT: poh lehn tah

WHAT IT SAYS: **porcini**

WHAT IT MEANS: an edible mushroom with a thick stem and a plump, round top

HOW YOU PRONOUNCE IT: pohr chee nee

WHAT IT SAYS: **primavera**

WHAT IT MEANS: made with fresh vegetables; usually refers to a cream sauce most often served with pasta

HOW YOU PRONOUNCE IT: pree muh vehr uh

WHAT IT SAYS: **prosciutto**

WHAT IT MEANS: a dry, spicy Italian ham, usually served in paper-thin slices

HOW YOU PRONOUNCE IT: proh shoo toh

WHAT IT SAYS: **quesadilla**

WHAT IT MEANS: a wheat tortilla folded and filled with a mixture of chicken or meat, vegetables, and cheese

HOW YOU PRONOUNCE IT: keh sah dee yah

WHAT IT SAYS: **quinoa**

WHAT IT MEANS: a weed, similar to wild rice, often served in place of rice or other grains

HOW YOU PRONOUNCE IT: keen wah

WHAT IT SAYS: **radicchio**

WHAT IT MEANS: a red or purple member of the bitter-flavored chicory family of salad greens

HOW YOU PRONOUNCE IT: rah dee kee oh

WHAT IT SAYS: **ricotta**

WHAT IT MEANS: a soft Italian cheese, similar in texture to cottage cheese

HOW YOU PRONOUNCE IT: rih kaht tuh

WHAT IT SAYS: **rigatoni**

WHAT IT MEANS: a ribbed pasta, cut into short, slightly curved tubes

HOW YOU PRONOUNCE IT: rig ah toh nee

WHAT IT SAYS: **risotto**

WHAT IT MEANS: a rich, smooth dish of rice, cooked slowly with broth and sprinkled with cheese

HOW YOU PRONOUNCE IT: rih saw toh

WHAT IT SAYS: **roux**

WHAT IT MEANS: a mixture of butter and flour, cooked over low heat and used as a base for many sauces, particularly in Cajun cooking

HOW YOU PRONOUNCE IT: roo

WHAT IT SAYS: **saltimbocca**

WHAT IT MEANS: thinly pounded veal cutlets, stuffed with ham and cheese, seasoned with sage, and served with a wine sauce

HOW YOU PRONOUNCE IT: sahl tihm boh kuh

WHAT IT SAYS: **sashimi**

WHAT IT MEANS: very thinly sliced raw fish

HOW YOU PRONOUNCE IT: sah shee mee

WHAT IT SAYS: **scampi**

WHAT IT MEANS: large shrimp sautéed in olive oil and garlic

HOW YOU PRONOUNCE IT: scam pee

WHAT IT SAYS: **seviche**

WHAT IT MEANS: raw fish "cooked" in a marinade of lime or lemon juice

HOW YOU PRONOUNCE IT: seh vee chay

WHAT IT SAYS: **shallot**

WHAT IT MEANS: a small mild-flavored onion

HOW YOU PRONOUNCE IT: shal uht

WHAT IT SAYS: **sherbet**

WHAT IT MEANS: a frozen, icy dessert made with milk or cream, egg whites, and flavored with fruit juice

HOW YOU PRONOUNCE IT: sher biht

WHAT IT SAYS: **sorbet**

WHAT IT MEANS: a frozen, icy dish, served as a palate refresher or as a dessert, differing from sherbet in that it does not contain milk (see *sherbet*)

HOW YOU PRONOUNCE IT: sor bay

WHAT IT SAYS: **sorrel**

WHAT IT MEANS: leafy salad greens with a distinctive lemony flavor

HOW YOU PRONOUNCE IT: sor uhl

WHAT IT SAYS: **soufflé**

WHAT IT MEANS: a feather-light dish made of egg yolks and stiffly beaten egg whites, served either as a main dish or a dessert

HOW YOU PRONOUNCE IT: soo flay

WHAT IT SAYS: **squab**

WHAT IT MEANS: a young, farm-raised pigeon

HOW YOU PRONOUNCE IT: skwahb

WHAT IT SAYS: **Szechuan**

WHAT IT MEANS: a style of Chinese cooking noted for its use of hot peppers and spices

HOW YOU PRONOUNCE IT: sehch wahn

WHAT IT SAYS: **tagliatelle**

WHAT IT MEANS: pasta cut into narrow ribbons

HOW YOU PRONOUNCE IT: tah lyah teh leh

WHAT IT SAYS: **tapas**

WHAT IT MEANS: small snacks, originating in Spain, served as appetizers

HOW YOU PRONOUNCE IT: tah pas

WHAT IT SAYS: **tapenade**

WHAT IT MEANS: a purée of capers, black olives, anchovies, and olive oil, used as a spread for canapés and hors d'oeuvres.

HOW YOU PRONOUNCE IT: ta puh nahd

WHAT IT SAYS: **tartare**

WHAT IT MEANS: raw steak, ground or cut into small strips, traditionally served with a raw egg as a garnish

HOW YOU PRONOUNCE IT: tar tar

WHAT IT SAYS: **terrine**

WHAT IT MEANS: a rough-textured pâté (see *pâté*)

HOW YOU PRONOUNCE IT: teh reen

WHAT IT SAYS: **timbale**

WHAT IT MEANS: a creamy mixture of meat or vegetables, cooked in a small cup-shaped mold

HOW YOU PRONOUNCE IT: tihm bah lay

WHAT IT SAYS: **tiramisù**

WHAT IT MEANS: an Italian dessert consisting of layers of sponge cake soaked with coffee or liquor, layered with mascarpone cheese, and topped with grated chocolate

HOW YOU PRONOUNCE IT: tih ruh mee soo

WHAT IT SAYS: **truffle**

WHAT IT MEANS: either a highly prized and pricey edible subterranean fungus or a rich, creamy chocolate

HOW YOU PRONOUNCE IT: truhf uhl

WHAT IT SAYS: **velouté**

WHAT IT MEANS: a smooth white sauce made with stock instead of milk

HOW YOU PRONOUNCE IT: veh loo tay

WHAT IT SAYS: **vinaigrette**

WHAT IT MEANS: a simple dressing of oil and vinegar, often flavored with mustard and garlic

HOW YOU PRONOUNCE IT: vihn uh greht

WHAT IT SAYS: **wasabi**

WHAT IT MEANS: a condiment, similar in flavor to horseradish, made from the root of an Asian plant

HOW YOU PRONOUNCE IT: wah sah bee

WHAT IT SAYS: **ziti**

WHAT IT MEANS: a medium-sized tubular pasta

HOW YOU PRONOUNCE IT: zee tee

Share and Share Alike

When dining in a restaurant, a lady and her dinner companion may wish to split an entrée between them, either for reasons of appetite or economy. In such cases, however, a lady is always wise to read the small print on the menu, because some restaurants add a surcharge if a dish is shared by two or more people. To avoid unpleasantness, she may simply ask the server, "We're thinking about sharing the beef Wellington. Do you think it will serve two people?" If the server and the establishment wish to preserve their integrity, the server will give an honest answer, saying, "Yes, couples share it quite often," or suggesting, "Yes, I think it probably could serve two, but you might like a salad or an appetizer to go along with it." If there is a charge for splitting beef Wellington between two diners, and if that policy is not noted on the menu, it is the server's responsibility to mention that fact at this point. It is highly unlikely that such a surcharge will actually double the cost of the entrée, but a lady should not be subjected to unpleasant surprises when she is presented with the bill.

5

The Job of Eating

Business Meals, All Day Long

Some of the most crucial moments in a lady's professional life may well take place over a meal. Whether she is being interviewed for a job, attempting to close a sale, or asking a wealthy acquaintance for a contribution to a political campaign or a charitable cause, poor table manners could very well mean the difference between getting a great new job or missing the chance of a lifetime, impressing a new client or embarrassing her employer. A lady knows that behaving herself at the table is part of her job, a central part of the work she does every day.

If a lady intends to
do business in a restaurant,
she always makes a reservation.

————

A lady shows up on time
for a business luncheon. She realizes
that being late is not only bad for
business—it is also rude behavior.

————

If her employer has established
a limit on a lady's entertainment
budget, she sticks to it.

————

Even if a lady's employer has
given her the go-ahead to splurge,
a lady does not abuse her boss's
generosity. She can "splurge"
without ordering the biggest
steak on the menu or the
rarest bottle of wine
in the cellar.

————

When a lady is being entertained
at a business luncheon or dinner,
she waits for her host or hostess
to take the lead before ordering the
most expensive entrée or the most
extravagant bottle of wine
on the menu.

———

If a lady's company does not
have a budget for elaborate
entertaining, the lady chooses a
restaurant where she is confident
the prices will not send the
company into bankruptcy.

———

When selecting a restaurant
for a business luncheon or dinner,
especially if she is not well
acquainted with her clients and their
taste in food, she makes her
reservation at an establishment with
a varied, mainstream menu.

———

If a lady intends to conduct formal business during a meal—and particularly if she requires flip-charts or PowerPoint presentations—she requests a private dining room.

———

A lady knows that it is her own behavior and her own professionalism—not the extravagance of the restaurant—that will impress her clients and make her company shine.

———

A lady does not overindulge simply because she is a guest, being entertained on another person's expense account. A lady never overindulges.

———

DOING BUSINESS

At a business breakfast, luncheon, or dinner, a lady's table manners remain as refined as if she were at a private dinner or a formal banquet. If she is invited to do business at the table, however, she makes it clear that she intends the occasion to be about the job at hand. She cuts through the chitchat in the most ladylike but straightforward way possible. It is not at all rude for her to pull a meandering conversation back on track with a simple, to-the-point question such as, "Now, Joanne, what about the Brinkley deal?"

Even if every one of her fellow diners decides to squander an opportunity to do business, a lady retains her dignity, her integrity, and her composure. She knows she need not play the good-old-boy game in order to get her work done. In the future, and if she has the option to do so, she may suggest that her clients or coworkers and she conduct their business over the conference table, perhaps with soda and sandwiches brought in for sustenance.

Extended dinner parties financed by corporate expense accounts, stoked by twenty-ounce steaks and fueled by liquor, are still a reality, but macho, cholesterol-chugging, three-martini luncheons are much less common than they used to be—especially since women have assumed more and more leadership roles in the corporate world.

If a business meal is held in the dining room of a restaurant, fine or not-so-fine, all the diners at the table turn off their cell phones. Or, at the very least, they turn their cell phones to the "vibrate" mode. As a gesture of consideration for diners at the nearby tables, as well as her own fellow diners, if a lady must talk on her cell phone, even about business matters, she leaves the table. The day is past when anybody was convinced of the urgent need for a diner to return, accept, or make a cell phone call in the middle of a restaurant.

At the end of a business breakfast, luncheon, or dinner, it is highly unlikely that a lady's clients will offer to help out with the bill. Once all the eating, drinking, coffee sipping, and deliberating are done, the hostess simply says to the server, "Give me the bill, please." It would be unusual, in the extreme, for her to encounter any protests or offers to share in the tip. If such offers should arise, though, she simply says, "No thanks. Parkley Sprockets is getting this."

INVITATIONS AT THE OFFICE

If a lady is invited to a dinner, or any other social occasion, by a coworker, she does not assume that everyone else in the office has been invited. Unless the invitation has been posted on the break-room bulletin board, or has been distributed via an office-wide e-mail, she does not take it upon herself to ask a fellow employee, "Did you get invited to the Postons' for Friday night?" or to say, "Guess I'll be seeing you at Sue and Larry's tomorrow."

A Lady on a Job Interview

On many occasions the job-interview experience may involve a meal—whether it is a breakfast, a luncheon, or a dinner. Such occasions allow a lady's potential employers to size up her personality and her social skills. They also allow the lady a glimpse into the corporate personality of the firm where she may be invited to work.

At job-interview meals, a few guidelines are worth remembering:

- A lady waits to follow the lead of her host, or others at the table, before she orders either food or drink.

- To prevent unsightliness in the midst of the interview process, a lady avoids ordering potentially sloppy dishes such as pasta—unless she is fully confident she can handle them without mishap.

- If the direction of the conversation seems to stray from the business at hand, the lady may attempt to redirect it by saying, "Multi-Net did awfully well last year, didn't it?"

- If her host suggests a restaurant where the lady cannot, may not, or wishes not to eat the food, she lets that fact be known as soon as possible. More often than not, however, she will not even be asked about her preferences before the location for a job-interview meal is established. In such cases, she does her best to find something on the menu she can eat.

- If the table conversation turns to topics that the lady finds unpleasant—or if jokes of a racist, ethnic, homophobic, or any other degrading nature crop up—she does not join in the conversation or pretend to find the jokes amusing. To preserve her own self-respect, she may choose to speak up, stating that she finds such comments offensive. Even if she chooses to remain silent, she will have learned an important lesson about the business where she may be asked to work. Such comments may, in fact, be a determining factor in her decision to accept or turn down the job offer.

- If a lady does not drink alcohol, she does not order alcohol, even if everybody else at the table is ordering it.

- On an interview, a lady is always well advised to monitor her alcohol intake. Even if her interviewers are in their cups, they will have second thoughts about an interviewee who must be folded into a taxi at the end of the evening.

6

STAND UP AND BE FED

COCKTAIL PARTIES AND BUFFET SUPPERS

Buffets and cocktail parties offer some of life's most convivial experiences. On many occasions no formal dining table is involved, and guests are expected to stroll about, enjoying the company of good friends or getting to know new acquaintances. This does not mean, however, that such events are not without their almost unique challenges. They may demand that a lady figure out how to juggle a plate and a beverage, balancing both of them on her lap. At such parties, in fact, a lady's social skills may be put to the toughest test, but these events may also offer her some of the best times of her party-going life.

At a cocktail supper, or
any occasion where hors d'oeuvres
and canapés have been set out for the
guests, a lady does not sort through
the snacks in search of the most
luscious or largest morsel. Neither
does she pick out all the cashews
from the mixed nuts.

—

If a lady is hosting a
cocktail party, she invites only as
many people as can comfortably
enjoy themselves in her home.

—

If a lady is hosting
a cocktail party where she
provides alcohol, she must
also provide food.

—

When hosting any event
where alcohol is provided,
a lady always provides
nonalcoholic options.

—

A lady does not attend a party to which she has not been specifically invited—unless she is assured that the host has insisted that all her friends "bring anybody" they know.

—

At a buffet dinner, once a lady has filled her plate to an appropriate level, she need not wait for all the other guests to wend their way through the line before she begins eating. In such situations, however, she waits until at least a couple of other guests have filled their plates and joined her. She does not dine alone.

—

Even if she is not well acquainted with anyone else in the room, once she has filled her plate, a lady seats herself near another guest, or a group of guests, and attempts to begin a conversation, either by introducing herself or by saying, "My, isn't this pork roast beautiful?"

—

A lady does not
station herself by the food table
at a cocktail party, feeding herself
off the serving platters.

—

A lady never places her
glass or her coffee cup directly
on a piece of furniture, even if that
piece of furniture is a glass-top coffee
table. She knows that a sweaty glass
will leave damp rings even on glass or
stone, while the heat from hot coffee
will leave circles of steam on
any surface.

—

If a lady is offered a coaster
or a cocktail napkin, she uses it.

—

If a lady is not offered a
coaster or a cocktail napkin,
she asks for one.

———

STANDING INVITATIONS

While a sit-down dinner party for eight
or ten people can be one of life's loveliest
experiences, a lady may find that such occasions
are increasingly rare today. Instead, more often
than not, she will find herself invited to a sizable
"cocktail supper" with a substantial spread of
hors d'oeuvres and canapés, or she will discover
that the evening's repast has been spread out on
a sideboard or on the dining room table. Earlier
in the day, if a lady is invited for brunch, she
will probably be right to assume that a buffet of
rich egg-based casseroles, breads, bacon,
sausage, and fruit awaits her. In such situations,
she is expected to serve herself and find her own
place to settle in the living room, den, or even
on a convenient staircase.

Such occasions allow the host or hostess to
entertain a goodly number of friends on a
single occasion. Thus, a lavish buffet may turn
out to be a considerably grander experience

than a sit-down dinner, with much milling about and lively chatter. In such situations, although the spirit of the evening may be somewhat casual, a lady does not assume, simply because she must fill her own plate, that she may let her good manners lapse.

At any cocktail supper or buffet dinner, a lady must greet her host or hostess immediately upon her arrival. Within seconds, if the party is being run correctly, she will be offered a drink, by her host or hostess or by a server. If a full bar is available, she may be asked, "May I get you something to drink?" If the offerings are less varied, she will be asked, "Would you like a glass of wine?" or "May I get you a beer?" If a lady does not drink alcohol, she simply says, "I'd love a soda or a glass of water, if that's available."

During the cocktail hour, a lady's goal is to make pleasant conversation with her fellow guests. (She does not attempt to monopolize her host or hostess.) She may strike up a chat with any other guest, particularly if she and the other guest find themselves standing in line at the bar or side by side in the buffet line. No matter how enjoyable that conversation, however, a lady and her fellow guest do not linger at the bar or at the serving table so long as to impede the flow of traffic. They take their drinks or fill their plates, and then move out into the larger world of the party.

At a cocktail supper, or even the simplest cocktail party, a lady may find a great variety of bite-sized foods. If a stack of small plates is offered, she takes one and proceeds to make her selection from the table. Especially if she is consuming alcohol, a lady is well advised to enjoy a substantial selection of the treats that are offered to her. She does not, however, load her plate to overflowing, giving the impression that she has not eaten all day—or that she is intent on taking undue advantage of her host or hostess's hospitality. The same applies to her consumption of alcohol, if it is offered.

At a buffet supper or at a brunch, a lady will find plates, knives, forks, and napkins arranged on the buffet table, ready for her use. In some cases the plates will be at one end of the buffet table, with the flatware (wrapped in napkins) at the other end. In other cases, both the plates and the flatware will be set out at the start of the buffet line, thus requiring the lady to perform a nimble juggling act as she proceeds through the line. As she approaches the buffet line, a lady keeps her wits about her, taking her place in line and following in the direction in which the other guests seem to be moving. She understands that all her food, including the salad, entrée, and side dishes, are expected to go on her one dinner plate. Separate plates will be offered for dessert, but only later in the evening. Even if the dessert is already set out on a sideboard, a lady understands that she will have the opportunity to return later in the evening to enjoy that treat.

At a large party, a lady may discover that duplicate dishes have been set out on both sides of the table. If such is the case, she takes her servings from one side of the table. She does not find it necessary to check out the other side of the table, in hopes of finding better cuts of tenderloin or more luscious slices of the chocolate truffle cake.

At the best of all possible buffets, at the end of the serving line a lady will be offered a lap tray, sizable enough to hold her plate, her flatware, and her glass. Once she has found a place where she can comfortably sit, she settles herself in and balances her tray on her lap. If she finds that her glass seems to sit unsteadily on her tray, she places her glass on some convenient flat surface, provided that surface is unlikely to be damaged by the bottom of a damp glass. When all else fails, a lady places her glass on the floor beside her, keeping it within ready reach and watching out for unintentionally clumsy guests.

If lap trays are not offered, a lady simply spreads her napkin on her lap and balances her plate on top of it. She takes special care not to saw away at her food with her knife and fork, lest she send a chunk of pork roast sailing across the room.

A lady may return to the buffet for a second helping, if she desires one. She does not allow herself to be seen scraping the bottom of the casserole dish, however. If fresh plates are still available on the table or the sideboard, she may take one, or she may serve herself on the dinner plate she is already using, just as if she were in her own home. When serving herself from a buffet in a public restaurant, however, she remembers that health department guidelines most likely will require that she take a fresh plate each time she returns to the buffet table.

When it is time for dessert, the host or hostess, or a server, probably will come through the room, picking up dinner plates and used flatware. If her fellow diners all seem to have finished eating, a lady surrenders her plate as well. She does not say, "Wait a minute, I'm still eating my chicken." Dessert may then be served to her on an individual plate, or her host or hostess may say, "There's fresh peach cobbler in the dining room. I hope you'll try it."

Once all the trays have been picked up and the plates have been cleared away, a lady may linger among her fellow guests for as long as she pleases, provided it does not appear that she will be the last guest to be shooed out the door. Whenever she makes her departure, a lady makes sure to bid farewell directly to her host or hostess, thanking them for their hospitality and for their kindness in including her in a lovely occasion. If the party has been hosted by a number of people, the lady need only say "thank you" and "good night" to one or two of her hosts or hostesses. She makes a particular effort to express her thanks to the owners of the house where the party is taking place. When a party has been hosted by a number of people, she sends her thank-you note to the host or hostess who graciously welcomed a houseful of guests into his or her home.

How to Set Up a Buffet

When a lady serves a buffet-style meal in her own home, she carefully arranges the table so that her guests can comfortably serve themselves. She includes everything they will need to enjoy their meal and provides easy access to the food (preferably positioning the table in the middle of the room).

Whether the buffet is a table set against the wall, a table in the middle of the room, or the

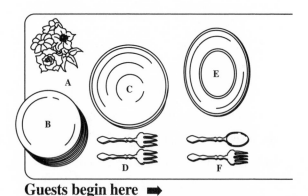

Guests begin here ➡

A. Floral Arrangement (optional)
B. Plates
C. Salad
D. Salad Utensils
E. Entrée
F. Serving Utensils

kitchen counter, guests will move alongside it in a single line. Accordingly, a lady stacks the plates at the beginning of the line and places the flatware, rolled in napkins, at the end of the line, which gives guests a free hand to serve themselves.

The lady places a serving spoon or fork with every dish on the buffet. She may serve beverages from a separate table. Flowers are a nice touch, provided they do not take up too much room.

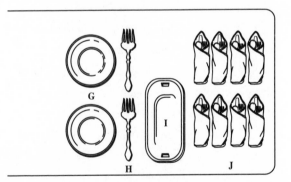

G. Side Dishes
H. Serving Utensils
I. Bread Platter
J. Flatware/Napkins

GATHERING THE GROUP

A good host attempts to give her guests plenty of notice. Two weeks lead time is appropriate for a dinner party. One week is sufficient for a more casual gathering.

Whether she offers her invitation in writing or by phone, she makes sure to answer all the questions her guests might logically have. For written invitations, a lady makes sure to include the nature of the party (cocktails, supper, brunch, a birthday party for Sue Ellen, or whatever), the date, the hour, the address, specifics about what to wear, and the information her guests need in order to reply. If her guests will need instructions about parking, she includes those as well.

If a hostess needs an accurate head count, she requests a reply by writing either "RSVP" or, more directly, "Please reply" at the bottom of her invitation, making sure to include her phone number. If her prospective guests have not responded by a reasonable time (forty-eight hours before the party), she may gracefully ask whether or not they plan to attend.

7

The Ghastly Table

Dealing with Dining Disasters

At any time, in a restaurant or at a private dinner party, a lady may discover that something unattractive or inedible is stuck between her teeth, or she has put some inedible morsel in her mouth. At such moments she need not feel debilitating embarrassment. The solution is, in fact, quite simple. If the objectionable morsel may be removed with her fork or spoon, that's the utensil she uses. If she can use her fingers to clean an errant string of spinach from her lips, she does so, using her napkin to mask her action and then disposing of the unsightly item on her plate. She feels no need to mention her difficulty to her dinner companions. Such unpleasantness, after all, is likely to be part of any lady's life.

Other problems may arise, however.

IF A LADY DISCOVERS SHE HAS SPILLED SOUP OR
GRAVY OR ANY OTHER SAUCE ON HER BLOUSE,
DRESS, SKIRT, OR SLACKS . . .

Even if she is dining among her closest
friends or family members, and even if they are
dining in a private home, a lady excuses herself
from the table, offering no explanation—not
even a self-effacing one such as, "Well, look
what a mess I've made of myself." In the
bathroom, she assesses the damage. If she has
soiled her dress, she uses a napkin, dampened
with a bit of cold water to attempt to remove or
at least lessen the stain. Even if she cannot
remove the stain at that very moment, she will
at least make it easier for the dry cleaner or the
washing machine to remove it the next day.

If a lady discovers a dribble of soup or sauce
on her blouse, however, she must be much more
careful. In almost every case, after excusing
herself from the table and reaching the bathroom,
she blots the stain lightly with a napkin or a bit

of tissue. If she is particularly savvy and is fully confident that she knows whether the stain is oil based or wine or water based, she may attempt to rub the stain briskly—using a tiny bit of warm water if the stain is oil based, or cold water if no grease is involved. In either case, however, a lady takes a great risk of spoiling a favorite blouse.

If she finds herself in a lady's room where an attendant is on hand, she may simply say, "Looks as if I've done some damage here. What do you think I should do?" The attendant may, in fact, be knowledgeable about removing stains and may have fabric-cleaning supplies on hand. If she does not solve the lady's problem—or even if she makes the problem worse—the lady does not complain. She has, after all, asked for the assistance, with no guarantee that it will work. In any case, if the attendant has attempted to fix the problem, the lady offers a grateful gratuity before returning to the party.

Should a lady notice that another diner has dropped a bit of soup or sauce on his or her clothing, the lady simply says, ever so quietly, "Lynn, I believe you've got a bit of Hollandaise sauce on your jacket." It is precisely the same courtesy a lady offers to a friend whose blouse has accidentally become unbuttoned.

IF A LADY DISCOVERS A PROBLEM WITH THE BILL IN A RESTAURANT . . .

Although a lady does not pull out a calculator, or a pad and pencil, she is not ashamed to review the bill in a restaurant before she pays it. If she discovers that she has been overcharged, or undercharged, she calls the server discreetly to her side and points out the error. If there have been problems with the service earlier in the evening—for example, if an entrée has been unacceptable and the server has assured the guest that there will be no charge for it or that a complimentary dessert will be provided—and that correction is not noted on the bill, a lady points out that error as well. If the server immediately goes about correcting the error, the lady simply assumes the error is a human foible. If the server attempts to argue with the lady, the lady asks to see a manager.

IF A LADY'S CREDIT CARD IS DECLINED IN A RESTAURANT . . .

In such situations a lady does not call attention to an already awkward state of affairs. She does not leap to the defensive, proclaiming, "Well, I'm sure there's a huge credit limit on that card," "I paid that bill over a month ago," or "Somebody's computer must be screwed up." Instead, she leaves the table along with the server, asking, "Would you mind running the card through again?" Even if the lady is confident that her credit is good, if the card continues to be declined, and if she does not have enough ready cash to cover the bill and the tip, she asks if she may pay by check, visit the nearest ATM, or return the next day with cash. If the establishment declines any and all of these— and if she is not offered the option of washing dishes to work off the debt—the lady has no recourse except to return to the table and throw herself upon the mercy of her friends, who will probably agree to chip in, if their own finances permit. A lady repays their kindness within the next twenty-four hours, repaying them in cash. A lady does not let such debts linger.

IF A LADY DROPS FOOD ON THE TABLECLOTH OR ON THE FLOOR . . .

A lady does not call attention to the situation by exclaiming, "Oops!" or "Clumsy me!" If she has dropped a sizeable chunk of food or a considerable amount of sauce, her only recourse is to use her napkin to retrieve the dropped food or to blot up the sauce. She hopes that her host or hostess will be alert enough to say, "Thank you, Ellen, for taking care of that. Let me get you a fresh napkin." If such is not the case, she alerts her host or hostess, or a server, saying, "Excuse me, but I believe I could use a fresh napkin." When the fresh napkin is provided, a lady makes no further explanation, exchanging it, without comment, for the soiled linen.

IF A LADY BELCHES, AUDIBLY, AT THE DINNER TABLE . . .

A lady realizes that the frailties of the flesh may creep up on any one of us, at any time. A lady may use her napkin to stifle a discreet burp, but if a loud frog-croaking belch overcomes her, she must simply say, "Excuse me, please." A lady may only be forgiven for such unpleasantness once during a meal, however. If she discovers that she has been overcome by indigestion, she must head for the bathroom, in search of a sip of water. Her next option is to ask her host or hostess for a glass of soda water. (Asking for an antacid tablet probably will not solve the problem immediately.) Her final recourse is simply to inform her host or hostess, and her spouse or date, that she must depart, offering her regrets as sincerely and as expeditiously as possible.

IF A LADY KNOCKS OVER A GLASS OF WATER,
WINE, OR ICED TEA, OR A CUP OF COFFEE . . .

If no breakage has occurred, a lady's first
instinct is to grab her napkin and attempt to
sop up the mess. Her dinner companions may
offer their napkins as well, and a lady gladly
accepts that assistance. If she is in a private
home, her host or hostess will probably rise to
help clean up. If she is in a well-attended
restaurant, a server will materialize, almost out
of nowhere, to provide assistance. If the spillage
involves red wine, strong iced tea, or coffee, her
host or hostess may attempt a quick application
of cold water to the stain.

In any case, though, a lady can do nothing
except say, "Excuse me for making such a mess."
She assumes that her host or hostess, or the
server, will provide her and her fellow guests with
fresh napkins. A thoughtful host or hostess—or a
responsible server—will provide a clean napkin to
cover the damp stain on the table.

On the way out the door, or when she writes her thank-you note, the lady may remember to say, "I hope you'll forgive my clumsiness with the wine glass." Otherwise, she says nothing more. Such accidents are an almost inevitable part of entertaining, or being entertained.

IF A LADY FINDS THE FOOD IN A RESTAURANT INEDIBLE OR THE DRINKS UNDRINKABLE . . .

It makes no difference whether she is paying for her own dinner or whether she is another person's guest. There is no reason why a lady must soldier on, gnawing her way through a semi-raw steak or a stringy breast of chicken. She makes no apology for telling the server, "I'd like my steak cooked medium, not medium rare, please," or "My chicken is overcooked—would you ask the chef to try again, please?" If it appears that the lady's steak, once it returns, has simply been reheated under the microwave, the lady remains firm, saying, "I'd like a fresh steak.

Please do not reheat this one." If the problem continues, she asks to speak to a manager.

The same advice applies if a lady finds her cocktail too weak, her coffee overbrewed, or her tea too strong. As a patron of the restaurant, she has a right to ask for her food to be served the way she wants it. If she learns, however, that a particular establishment's food is not cooked or served the way she prefers, she avoids that establishment in the future, thus saving herself, and the establishment, any further anguish.

IF A LADY'S CHILDREN ARE MISBEHAVING,
EITHER AT A RESTAURANT OR AT A DINNER IN A
PRIVATE HOME . . .

It is every parent's prerogative to discipline children in the way he or she sees fit. In public places or at a dinner party, brunch, luncheon, or luau, however, a lady recognizes that her children's misbehavior may very likely disrupt the meal for her dinner companions or the other diners in the restaurant—even if it is a fast-food establishment. In such cases, a lady does not attempt to discipline her child in public, thus risking the possibility that fellow diners will be asked to share in even more unpleasantness. Instead, she takes the child away from the table, exercising appropriate discipline in a restroom, in the corner of a parking lot, or in the family automobile. If the child will not amend his or her behavior, or bursts into loud wails, a lady asks her server to provide to-go boxes for the food of all her family members. Once the food has been packed up, the lady, her child, and the rest of the family depart as swiftly and as discreetly as possible.

IF AN ARGUMENT OCCURS AT THE DINNER TABLE . . .

A lady enjoys friends who have strong opinions, but she also knows that out-and-out arguing does not aid digestion. If she discovers that the conversation is threatening to grow contentious, she simply says, "Now, friends, let's

change the subject." If she is the hostess at a
sizable dinner party, she may have to rise from
her seat and play referee. If her guests refuse to
behave themselves, she may even ask that they
change seats, simply to get away from each other.

If the argument seems to have been fueled
by alcohol, the lady suggests that they abstain
from any further drinking. In the worst possible
circumstances, when the enjoyment of her
other guests or other people in a restaurant is
threatened, a lady may be forced to say, "Tom
and Tammy, I'm afraid this is getting out of hand.
I must ask you either to end this conversation, or
take it to the sidewalk." If the problem continues,
without choosing sides, the lady must ask both
of her argumentative friends to leave.

IF A LADY DROPS A STEAK ON THE KITCHEN
FLOOR OR ON THE DECK BESIDE THE GRILL . . .

Nobody need know what happens in the
privacy of a lady's own kitchen. If she is
cooking in the presence of her guests, however,

she must express at least some concern over a steak that has slipped off the spatula and onto the gravel. If a replacement steak is available, she says, "I'm afraid this one is headed to the garbage." If no replacement is available, she suggests that she and another guest (preferably her date or a very close friend) share one of the larger steaks. She may be perfectly willing to take the gravel-encrusted steak to the kitchen, rinse it off, and grill it for herself. Unfortunately, some of her guests may find even that solution absolutely unpalatable.

IF A LADY DISCOVERS THAT THE UTENSILS SET BEFORE HER ARE DIRTY . . .

If a lady is dining in a restaurant, she simply asks her server for replacements, saying, "I don't think this spoon is quite clean. May I have another?" In such circumstances, when a lady is a guest in a private home, she faces an additional challenge. Still, she attempts to call as little attention as possible to the awkward moment.

After taking her place at the table, she does not immediately inspect the flatware and then declare, "Otto, it looks like you need to run this spoon through the dishwasher again." Instead, once her food has been put before her, she simply asks her host, "Otto, could I have a fresh salad fork?" The lady hopes that, when Otto comes to replace the salad fork, he will check to make sure the other flatware is in better shape.

If a lady wishes to play games, she may choose to drop the soiled utensil on the floor, thus creating an excuse for requesting a replacement. Unfortunately, if the dinner knife and the dessert fork are soiled as well, she may end up requiring her host or hostess to run a relay race between the dinner table and the silver chest.

IF A LADY IS PRESENTED WITH FOOD SHE CANNOT EAT . . .

A lady attempts to prevent this sort of awkwardness, for herself and for her host or hostess, by paying attention to what might be

served to her. If she has food allergies, when
she is invited for dinner, she makes it a point to
inform her host or hostess, saying, "It's probably
best to tell you I have a food allergy. I'm allergic
to nuts [or shellfish or flour]. But otherwise I
can eat anything." A lady trusts that her host or
hostess will be grateful for her frankness.

When she sits down at the table, nevertheless,
a lady may still be served a course she cannot eat.
She may leave the food untouched, or she may
simply decline to take any of it when it is offered
to her. She may choose to eat a bit of bread and
butter, but if her host or hostess asks her,
"Hayley, is there something wrong?" she replies
truthfully by simply saying, "This looks lovely,
but I can't eat shellfish." Her host or hostess then
attempts to provide an alternative course.

If a lady's religion restricts her from eating
any dish, however, she makes no pretense. If
her host or hostess asks her why she is not
eating the shrimp cocktail, she says, "Thanks,
but I don't eat shellfish." She does not say,

"Sorry, but I don't eat shellfish." A lady does not apologize for her beliefs.

On the other hand, if a lady simply does not care for the food placed before her, she finds something else on the plate that she can eat, or she takes a couple of bites of the lamb chop, even if she hates lamb.

If a lady becomes ill at the table . . .

Perhaps it's because of the salmon (that wasn't sufficiently smoked) or the hot asparagus soup (that wasn't quite hot enough) or the pork roast (that wasn't roasted to 160 degrees). Or maybe it's the leftover tuna sandwich that she had for lunch earlier in the day. For whatever reason, if a lady finds herself ill, either at a private dinner or in a restaurant, she must leave the table immediately, heading for a bathroom. If she feels no better after visiting the bathroom, she informs her host or hostess that she must leave, and her spouse or date must depart with her.

Meanwhile, in the most horrific of all

circumstances, a lady may be overtaken by sudden nausea, actually become sick to her stomach, and even throw up at the table. Such moments steal up on even the best-mannered lady. She may inevitably feel embarrassed by the moment, but unless her illness has been brought on by overindulgence, she feels no personal guilt. She is remorseful and assists her host or hostess in straightening up the table, if she feels well enough to do so. In most cases, however, she will be better advised to retreat to the bathroom, wipe her face with a cool towel, and depart as quickly as possible.

In writing her thank-you note for the evening, a lady does not avoid the reality of what has taken place. Instead, she states frankly, "Your dinner party was lovely. I hope my illness did not ruin the evening for you and your other guests." In such instances, a lady may wish to accompany her thank-you note with a small bouquet of flowers. If her illness persists, however, her host or hostess may wish to send her a get-well note.

IF A LADY SUSPECTS, IN THE AFTERMATH OF A
DINNER PARTY, THAT SHE HAS FOOD POISONING . . .

If a lady finds herself ill after a private dinner
party, cooked by the hosts themselves, she can
do little except let bygones be bygones. (If such
illness becomes a regular occurrence after dinner
in a particular home, however, a lady may
rethink accepting invitations to that house.) She
may mention her illness to the other guests, to
ascertain whether it is her stomach that is at
fault, or the food. But nothing is accomplished
by calling her host or hostess and saying, "Last
night was great, but I ended up spending six
hours in the emergency room."

If the food has been provided by a caterer,
however, the lady does let her hosts know that
there has been a problem. The same advice
applies if she has dined in a restaurant and has
become ill afterward. Professional caterers and
restaurants are expected to abide by strict
health department regulations if they are to

keep their licenses. The lady may elect not to patronize a restaurant, should she be suspicious of its cleanliness. But her host or hostess must be informed if it appears that a caterer's food has made her ill, so that they may refrain from using that catering company again.

IF A LADY EVEN SUSPECTS THAT ONE OF HER DINNER COMPANIONS IS CHOKING AND IS IN NEED OF ASSISTANCE . . .

If a dinner companion begins choking on her food, and continues to do so, even for a split second, a lady springs into action. If the lady knows how to apply the Heimlich maneuver, she does so. If she is not trained in the Heimlich maneuver, however, she does not risk causing further damage by applying her personal version of the maneuver. If she is in a restaurant, where servers are usually trained to help in such situations, she calls for assistance, loudly and firmly. If she is at a private dinner party, and if no other guest rises to the occasion, she calls out, "Does anybody here know the Heimlich?" (In this instance, a lady is allowed to shout if needed.) If there is no response, and unless she knows some certain other means of loosening an obstruction from the windpipe, she calls 911 and asks for immediate assistance. She does not assume that she can drive the choking victim to the emergency room in her own car.

A lady is best advised to consult her local chapter of the American Red Cross for thorough training in the Heimlich maneuver. She does not assume that she knows how to save a life simply because she has seen a step-by-step chart in a restroom.